Praise for the Yarn

"If you haven't read this series yet, I highly recommend giving it a go. The mystery will delight you, and afterward you'll be itching to start a knitting or crochet project of your own."

—Cozy Mystery Book Reviews

"A cozy mystery that you won't want to put down. It combines cooking, knitting and murder in one great book!"

—Fresh Fiction

"The California seaside is the backdrop to this captivating cozy that will have readers heading for the yarn store in droves."

—Debbie's Book Bag

Praise for Betty Hechtman's National Bestselling Crochet Mysteries

"Will warm the reader like a favorite afghan."

—National bestselling author Earlene Fowler

"Get hooked on this new author . . . Who can resist a sleuth named Pink, a slew of interesting minor characters and a fun fringe-of-Hollywood setting?"

—Crochet Today!

"Fans . . . will enjoy unraveling the knots leading to the killer."

—Publishers Weekly

"Classic cozy fare . . . Crocheting pattern and recipe are just icing on the cake."

—Cozy Library

Praise for the Writer for Hire Mysteries

"Plenty of plot twists and an appealing heroine with a reluctant love interest. What's not to like?"

—*Kirkus Reviews*

"A sympathetic heroine coping with her own losses and colorful characters from a writer's group combine nicely with an intriguing plot involving class and abuse. Readers will look forward to future installments."

—*Publishers Weekly*

Books by Betty Hechtman

Yarn Retreat Mysteries

Yarn to Go
Silence of the Lamb's Wool
Wound up in Murder
Gone with the Wool
A Tangled Yarn
Inherit the Wool
Knot on Your Life
But Knot for Me
Knot a Game

Crochet Mysteries

Hooked on Murder
Dead Men Don't Crochet
By Hook or By Crook
A Stitch in Crime
You Better Knot Die
Behind the Seams
If Hooks Could Kill
For Better or Worsted
Knot Guilty
Seams Like Murder
Hooking for Trouble
On the Hook
Hooks Can Be Deceiving
One for the Hooks

Writer for Hire Mysteries

Murder Ink
Writing a Wrong

Knot a Game

BETTY HECHTMAN

BEYOND THE PAGE
PUBLISHING

Knot a Game
Betty Hechtman
Copyright © 2022 by Betty Hechtman

Beyond the Page Books
are published by
Beyond the Page Publishing
www.beyondthepagepub.com

ISBN: 978-1-958384-94-7

Chapter 1

What could Madeleine Delacorte possibly want to see me about that was so important? The voicemail she'd left had sounded more like a summons than an invitation for a friendly cup of coffee. As much as I'd come to think of Madeleine as a friend, we were not exactly on a level playing field. She and her sister Coral were like the local royalty in Cadbury by the Sea, California. And I was still struggling to make a go of the Yarn Retreat business I'd inherited from my late aunt. She didn't talk about her age, but I guessed she was in her late sixties. I tried to be vague about my age too as I turned toward forty and just said mid-thirties. One thing we had in common was a connection to Vista Del Mar. Her family owned the hotel and conference center, and I used it to host what I'd recently branded as "weekends devoted to yarn craft, camaraderie and more."

I hoped it didn't mean that Madeleine and Cora had rethought the sweetheart deal they had generously continued to offer me when I took over the business after my Aunt Joan died. Plainly put, that deal was the only way I could continue doing the retreats.

As it was, I still needed to supplement my income by being the dessert chef for a local restaurant and baking muffins for the coffee places in Cadbury by the Sea. I had grown to love putting on the retreats even though I'd started out on shaky ground, barely knowing the difference between knitting and crochet, let alone how to do either of them. I had gotten pretty good with hooks and needles, though I did always have help with the workshops. Just as I was beginning to see my way, I didn't want to get shut down.

Now I was just anxious to get the answer. I shut my kitchen door and headed across the street and through the stone pillars that marked the entrance to Vista Del Mar. I had to remind myself that it was August. You couldn't tell by the weather. It was always the same—cool and cloudy. The morning air smelled of the ocean mixed with the smoke from all the fireplaces. There was at least one in every building of the hotel and conference center left from the days when they were the only source of heat. The moody-looking Arts and Crafts–style buildings were spread over a hundred or so acres of slopes studded with Monterey pines and Monterey cypress trees here on the tip of the Monterey Peninsula. The oldest of the buildings were over one hundred years old and left from its origin as a young women's camp.

It felt a little like leaving the world behind. There was a timeless quality about the place and from where I was standing it could have been the early 1900s, the 1950s, now or anytime in between. The grounds were largely left to grow as they chose, or to die for that matter. When one of the lanky pines keeled over, it was left in place to decompose undisturbed. There were rumors that the same was true for any wildlife that met their maker in the scruffy brush around the trees.

I was already supposing what I would do if Madeleine pulled the plug on the yarn retreats. After all, when I'd first come to Cadbury and moved into my aunt's guesthouse, I'd thought it was temporary—just long enough for me to get my life together. I was at a low point and it had been that or move back in with my parents. At thirty-something, moving back home was too embarrassing.

I always assumed I'd go back to Chicago. But when my aunt died everything changed. She'd left her house and business to me to deal with. Though even then, I had a niggling feeling once I got everything settled, I would want to move on. I had a whole history of short-lived pursuits.

I hadn't expected to put down roots here. It had just sort of happened without my noticing. I moved out of the guesthouse and into the main house and made friends while I tried to continue her business. Then there was Dane Mangano. He was my neighbor and so much more. I had tried to steer clear of a relationship but his persistence had won out and pushed us beyond being just friends. I blushed just thinking of his visit the night before. I was still trying to keep our status from the small-town gossips, with little success. And in the back of my mind, I wondered if it was all about the chase and now that he'd won, he'd lose interest. Or maybe I hoped so.

But for now, I needed to deal with the appointment with Madeleine. I waved my hand, trying to fan away the leftovers of the blush as I neared the group of communal buildings that I considered the heart of Vista Del Mar. I wanted to appear cool and collected, not somebody thinking about a hot night with her boyfriend.

I was supposed to meet Madeleine at the café named for her and her sister inside the building called the Lodge. I always thought of it as being the heart of Vista Del Mar. It had been built as a social hall when the place was a camp. Now it was where guests came to check in and hang out.

I pulled open the door and went inside the cavernous space. There was no ceiling, just an open framework that held large chandeliers. At this time of the morning, it was quiet. The seating area around the massive fireplace was empty. No one was using the pool table or table tennis set up in the back. And all the board games were stacked on the shelf. The manager of the small gift shop had just opened the door adjacent to the game area and was putting out a rack of T-shirts to entice customers.

I waved at the clerk behind the massive wooden counter. Normally, I would have stopped to talk to Cloris, but I just wanted to get whatever awaited me over with.

The café was at the front near the wooden counter and a mirror image of the gift shop. The door was open and the smell of freshly brewed coffee wafted my way as I felt my anticipation grow.

Madeleine was sitting at a table by a window that looked out on the sand dunes at the edge of the property. The rest of the tables were empty. The barista had just set down a cup in front of Madeleine. By the froth on the top, I guessed it was a cappuccino, which surprised me. But then she was all about moving beyond her boundaries now. After all the years of being sheltered and having her choices restricted, she was open to trying out everything she had missed.

She'd started wearing her hair in a swingy bob cut and had it colored a honey blond. She'd gone from stodgy-looking outfits to wearing a lot of denim, so I was surprised to see her wearing a dark plaid suit and low-heeled shoes that had ties. The whole outfit looked very retro and made me even more uneasy.

Bob, the barista, smiled at me. "Your usual?" I nodded and he went back to the espresso machine to make me a mostly foam cappuccino.

"Good morning," I said to Madeleine as I pulled out a chair. "You wanted to see me," I added, getting right to it. I hoped the tension in my voice didn't show, not wanting to let on that my whole future might hinge on her answer.

She looked down at the large cup in front of her. "Do you think I should have asked for a sprinkle of cinnamon?"

I was stunned by the question. Would she really have summoned me to meet her to advise her on what to put on her cappuccino? I knew she was used to being coddled, but that seemed extreme even for her. "Go for it," I said. I got up and went to the counter and came back with a shaker of cinnamon and sprinkled some on the white foam. "Was that it?" I asked. "You wanted advice on your coffee drink?"

She laughed. "I'm not that helpless. There is something else I want to talk to you about. It's about the next retreat you put on."

A *dun da dun dun* went off in my head. Here we go, a speech about how they can't continue with the special deal, that it was a carryover from my aunt but not meant to be forever, blah, blah, blah. I girded for the bad news.

"I was thinking that while I have been doing all kinds of new things, stretching my horizons and going out in the world, I've never tried working." She looked at me to see if I understood. "And the natural thing to me seemed to be helping you with your retreats, or at least one."

I let out a little of my breath. She wasn't cutting off the deal, but I wasn't so sure about what she had in mind. The best thing was to let her talk and then figure out if I was going to object.

"I had this idea," she said brightly. "I thought why not make the weekend one of those murder mystery games. Everyone gets dressed up and there's a murder and clues. The guests would figure it out with the help of the lead detective, Mrs. Maple. My job would be being Mrs. Maple." She gestured toward her outfit to show how ready she was.

"Of course, there would be yarn craft," she continued. "Knitting, I think. It seems to go better with murder. I wouldn't expect any salary. I'd be like a volunteer partner."

"Oh," was all I could manage.

"I'd help with the planning. I already made a lot of notes." She pulled out a black leather notebook. "I think that October would be a good month for it. People are already thinking of spooky things with Halloween. We could give it a British feel with high tea and Welsh rarebit and such. You could bake some biscuits and sweets. I thought we could use the restaurant you work for to bring in the special food." Just as my dry cappuccino arrived, she looked across the table. "So, what do you think?"

She might have phrased it as a question, but I had a feeling I didn't have a choice of how to answer. "It's different than what I've done, but if that's what you want," I said, "I think it's great that you want to work with me. We can brainstorm about how to pull it off."

"I think my job was to come up with the idea and then to be the detective." She tore the sheet with her notes out of the binder and handed it to me. "You can have this to start with. I'm sure you can come up with the rest. You can let me know how it's going. And then I'll step back in as Mrs. Maple ready to help the group follow the clues during the actual retreat." She took a sip of the cappuccino and made a face. "I think I'll try the cocoa powder next time. I don't have time to drink it anyway. There's a luncheon to raise money for the butterfly sanctuary and I have to go home and change." She looked down at the outfit and chuckled. "Cora would have a fit if I showed up wearing this."

What had she just dropped in my lap?

Chapter 2

"You want help with what, Feldstein?" Frank said with a squeak in his voice. Frank Shaw was a PI and my last boss. It was just a temp job and I was either an assistant detective or a detective's assistant, depending on who you talked to. Either way, it was my favorite of jobs and I probably never would have left it or Chicago if Frank hadn't been low on funds.

I was sitting in my kitchen, having gone home directly after my conversation with Madeleine. Julius had fallen asleep on the table with his tail draped over my arm. I didn't know what to do with Madeleine's idea and had called Frank for help.

We had stayed in touch since I'd come to Cadbury. I looked at him as an advisor and I think he looked at me as an amusement. I could tell by the rustling of paper that I'd caught him at lunchtime, which in his case was almost always a hoagie overflowing with meat, cheese and hot peppers, doused in Italian dressing. All the sitting during surveillance coupled with a lot of donuts and big sandwiches had left Frank with a soft shape that had more resemblance to the Pillsbury Doughboy than to James Bond.

The rustling of the sandwich wrapping continued as I told him about what she thought her job was.

He let out a laugh. "Have you considered saying no?"

"You do understand that her family owns the place where I host the yarn retreats and it's only through her and her sister's generosity that I've been able to make the business profitable. She's in her late sixties but in some ways she's like somebody just turning twenty. At that age, people are all about trying their wings and don't have a lot of common sense. I can't say no. Somehow, I have to make it work out."

"Got it," he said between chews. "So what do you need? A murder scenario?"

"I was thinking something along the lines of Colonel Mustard did it with a candlestick in the library," I said, referring to the Clue board game. "Though since it's going to be connected to yarn craft, maybe it should be Colonel Mustard strangled her with a newly knitted scarf in the library. I think she has in mind something very Agatha Christie-ish. *Something brings a group of people together for a weekend and one of them has murder on the schedule.*"

"Too boring, Feldstein," Frank said with a chuckle. "You need some blood, some excitement, some drama. Otherwise, you might as well have them play one of those murder games in a box."

"How do you know about those?" I asked.

"Feldstein, I have to do something to amuse myself when I'm doing a surveillance. But we're not here to talk about me. You do realize you're going to need help with this."

"What do you mean?" I asked, suddenly uneasy.

"Even if you come up with the plot and clues, you'll still need people to play the parts of victim, killer and suspects. Your paying customers get to be the detectives, along with your Mrs. Maple." He let out a chortle as he said her name.

"Oh, you're right," I said, getting a sinking feeling as the immensity of what I'd agreed to became clear.

"I'm not one to give rah-rah speeches, but I know you've got this. Just like solving mysteries, the answers are right there in front of you." He let out another chortle. "Though I suppose it's a little like those kids' books with the Waldo character caught in the crowd. Everything is jumbled up and it's sometimes hard to see it."

"You know about Waldo?" I said, surprised. I knew about Waldo from my stint teaching at the private school. He was a goofy-looking character in a classic series of children's books. There were double-page illustrations with him hidden in a crowd of people doing amusing things. The puzzle was to find him.

"Hey, Feldstein, I know you've always thought of me as a suave experienced PI, but there are a lot of nooks and crannies about me you don't know."

"Then tell me about them, Frank," I said.

"Not going to ruin the mystery," he said. "And besides, you're just stalling." I could hear the rattle of paper on his end and knew he was getting ready to end the call. "Start with the basics. I'm sure you'll figure it out." He stopped abruptly and his tone changed. "Just one thing," Frank said in a warning voice. "Try to make sure no one really dies."

• • •

It was all still fermenting in my mind that night as I drove to the Blue Door to do my dessert making and muffin baking. I understood what Frank meant about starting with the basics, I just wasn't sure what the basics were. I lugged the recycled grocery bag with the supplies for the muffins up the stairs to the porch that ran along the side of the small Victorian-style house. I always tried to wait until the restaurant was closing and the chef had vacated what he considered his domain before I arrived.

Inside, Lucinda Thornkill was just giving a credit card receipt to a customer. She was wearing a white dress that I was sure had a designer label. Even at the end of the day, her makeup was still perfect. Her husband, Tag, was making the rounds of the tables that had already been set for the next day. He made an adjustment to each place setting as Lucinda watched. She held it together while the servers went out the door.

"You've got to stop doing that," she said. "It's making everyone nervous."

He looked at her as if he was baffled by her comment. "Didn't you see? None of the forks and knifes were perfectly parallel. I wouldn't be able to sleep if I left everything askew." He ran his hand through his brown hair, which was too thick for a man in his fifties. I'd thought it was a wig at first, but Lucinda had assured me it was all real.

"I think he's getting worse," she said to me in a low voice. Shaking her head with dismay, she picked up a stray menu and slipped it in the slot on the host stand. I could still see the printing on the back below a picture of the two of them. The headline was . . . *And They Lived Happily Ever After.* It was a fairy-tale story describing how they'd been each other's first love in high school and then gone their separate ways, but never forgot about each other. Years later they met at their high school reunion. He was a widower and she was divorced and sparks flew when they danced to "their" song. They'd gotten married and followed their shared dream to have a restaurant in a small town by the sea. She insisted that Tag had never been like this in high school, but somehow he'd gotten super finicky about silly things like knives being perfectly parallel and procedures being followed. Lucinda had laughed it off at first, but it was getting to her.

Frank's words came back to me about starting with the basics. Food was basic, wasn't it? Besides, she seemed to need a distraction. I pulled her aside and told her about Madeleine's request.

Lucinda choked back a laugh. "She really doesn't know what working means. Did she really say her job was being Mrs. Maple?" I nodded and then moved on to how the restaurant might be involved.

"She wants it to have a British touch with afternoon tea and such. She even said she wanted the Blue Door to provide the food."

Lucinda looked over at her husband, who was adjusting the chairs now. "We'll leave Tag out of it. But of course, I can handle that." She looked at the shopping bag. "I'll get him out of here so you can get started on your baking. You know it's become customary for diners to order one of your desserts before their entrée. It used to be that they just wanted it set aside, but mistakes happened and pieces of cake disappeared. Now they want it actually on their table while they eat their dinner. You are legendary, my dear," she said, giving my arm a pat before she rounded up her husband.

It might have been small, but it was a first step toward Madeleine's requests for the retreat. And it was reassuring to know that Lucinda was so agreeable about helping.

I let out a breath now that I had the place to myself. I turned on the soft jazz I liked in the background and instantly began to relax. The arrangement I had was that I made the desserts for the restaurant first and then baked the muffins from supplies I'd brought. I glanced toward the window that looked out on Grand Street as I took the bag of supplies back to the kitchen. The wide street divided by a strip of parkway ran through downtown Cadbury and I could see that most everything was already closed. There were only a few cars parked on the street. Most Cadburians were home thinking about going to sleep, while I still had a long way to go before I could even consider it.

Baking was like therapy for me and as I mixed up the carrot cake batter, I was already getting ideas about how I'd handle Madeleine's idea. The air smelled of cinnamon from the baking cakes as I scribbled down some notes about the mystery weekend. It could be considered putting the horse before the cart, but I'd come up with a name for the retreat—*A Murderous Yarn*. I could run some ads on social media aimed at mystery lovers along with an email blast to my list.

The cakes were cooling on a rack and I'd begun on the banana nut muffins when my thoughts trickled back to the main event. I had a big challenge. While my main concern was pleasing Madeleine, I also needed to please the guests. I didn't want someone posting a negative comment on one of my social media pages about how they felt neglected. What I really wanted was a great review in a travel magazine. As I mashed the bananas, I imagined what something like that would do for my business.

I started giving myself a pep talk, thinking of the different things I'd done and how I'd risen to the occasion. I'd tried law school and given up after a semester, but you could say that it was good I realized it quickly and cut my losses. I'd been a teacher at a private school, which I'd been good at, but it wasn't for me. I would have stayed baking for the bistro in Chicago if they hadn't closed. Then came the temporary jobs. Looking back, the temp jobs were good experience as I had to jump into a spot and adapt right away. I'd spritzed perfume in Macy's and handed out samples on Michigan Avenue dressed as a stick of gum. Working for Frank had been the easiest adjustment since my job was mostly making calls and being friendly so that people would give up information without realizing it. I always thought fondly of that job and of Frank.

I was deep in thought when a knock at the glass portion of the door startled me. Instinctively, I started to grab a frying pan as a weapon to protect myself from an intruder, but stopped myself as reality set in. First of all, intruders didn't knock. Then this was Cadbury, where street crime was minimal. And finally, it was common knowledge that I would be baking at the Blue Door every night but Saturday, and people stopped by unannounced. Particularly one person. I remembered that Dane was working the late shift and it was time for his break.

"Something smells good," Dane said, sniffing the air when I let him in. He was dressed in his midnight blue cop uniform sans jacket in his I'm-too-tough-to-get-cold mode. I expected him to hug me and when he didn't, I gave him a suspicious look.

"Already it's changing. You always used to give me a hug first thing. It was all about the chase," I said, shaking my head only half seriously.

"What? Because I didn't hug you? Do you really think that now that you're mine, I won't want you anymore?" His tone was all teasing.

"I'm not so sure about that *mine* thing," I said. "I like to think I'm my own person."

He laughed as he followed me through what had been the living room of the house but was now the main dining area. "And what comes next? A reminder that at any moment you might take up your mother's offer on cooking school in Paris or detective school in L.A. and you don't want to leave any broken hearts behind?"

"You're making light of it," I said. "But it's serious. I don't have a good history of sticking with things or people."

"As I told you before, I'm a tough cookie. Besides, you know that you're stuck on me." He struck a cocky pose and laughed. "I was waiting to hug you when we weren't in front of a window and might be seen. No reason to give any gossips driving by something to talk about."

"Thank you," I said. He didn't care so much about that, but he knew I did. We were in the kitchen by then and he held out his arms and gave me a greeting hug.

"Was it worth the wait?" he teased.

"Yeah, but all the stuff on your belt and the radio on your shoulder kind of got in the way."

"For me, too, but it goes with being a cop," he said with a shrug. "Maybe I can make up for it later."

Much as I was still trying to keep one foot out the door, it was hard to resist his charms. He was the complete package. To say he was hot was an understatement. He was in fabulous shape from all his jogging and karate practice. His dark eyes usually danced with a smile, at least when I saw him. But behind all the cute hotness was what really counted—his character. He'd been brought up by a single alcoholic mother with an unknown father. Not really brought up by, more like he'd brought up himself and his younger sister and had to take care of his mother, too. He was still taking care of both of them when they fell apart and showed up at his place. His idea of being a cop was stopping trouble before it happened and so he offered free karate lessons and plates of his amazing spaghetti to the bored local teens. He acted like a big brother handing out advice as well.

I had been brought up as an only child by two doctors and this apple had fallen far from the tree. I had more in common with my late Aunt Joan, who'd been the black sheep of the family. I joked that my love of baking might have come from having a cardiologist mother who thought cookies only came in white boxes from a bakery. She had always been amazed when I gave her a cookie I'd made that was still warm from the oven. My father was a pediatrician and more soft-spoken. Neither of them was exactly pleased with my life choices. I thought by now it wouldn't bother me that they didn't approve, but it still did.

"What's all this?" Dane said, seeing some notes on the counter.

I told him about Madeleine's "suggestion" for a retreat. I had her note and some ideas that I'd scribbled down.

"Wait until Lieutenant Borgnine hears about that," Dane said with an impish smile. "He's not going to like it."

I hadn't thought about how the retreat would affect anybody else. The lieutenant and I had a rather contentious relationship because I had managed to figure out a few murders in the small town. Having a fake murder at Vista Del Mar would hardly please him. He viewed murder as serious business. not a game for a bunch of yarn enthusiasts. But since it was Madeleine's idea, he couldn't really object.

"But I'd really rather talk about other things," Dane said as I gave him a cup of coffee. "Have you considered how silly it is that we live down the street from each other. Wouldn't it make more sense if we both stayed in one of the houses?"

"You mean live together," I said. My voice came out a little too shrill and I took a deep breath and tried to collect myself. I was still adjusting to the idea that we were a couple and all that it implied. "That's kind of a big step." I left the thought hanging.

"Think about it," he said as he drained the cup. "In the meantime, I could come by your place for a *special breakfast* when I get off my shift."

"I hope that includes food," I said, and he laughed.

"I'll go to Sand City and pick up some breakfast sandwiches." He gave me a quick kiss on the cheek before heading off into the night to protect the mean streets of Cadbury.

Chapter 3

Frank was right. I needed to deal with the basics first. The most basic of all was setting things up with Vista Del Mar. I'd already decided to keep the number of guests small, but I'd need rooms that were together, a meeting room and space for the afternoon teas that Madeleine had mentioned. October wasn't that far away and I had to make sure the space was available.

I waited until Dane had gone home to catch up on his sleep the next morning and then I got myself together to go across to Vista Del Mar. I chose a time when I had the best chance of finding Cloris behind the registration counter. It was never a pleasure to deal with Kevin St. John. His title was manager, but he seemed to view himself as more of the lord of Vista Del Mar. He had been trying to take over the yarn retreats since I had put on the first one. He wasn't happy with the deal the Delacorte sisters continued to give me and that I was friends with them. He made things difficult for me whenever he could. He really needed to get a life outside the place. But I wasn't going to be the one to tell him.

There was a slight delay in my leaving. Julius started circling through my ankles as I walked to the door. Or tried to walk. I knew what the black cat was up to even before he made a pivot and went to the refrigerator. I started to protest that I'd already given him his morning snack of what I'd come to call stink fish, but the one thing I'd learned about cats since he'd come to live with me was they called the shots.

"Just this once," I said, putting down my purse. Who was I kidding? The cat knew how to work me. I held my nose in preparation as I opened the refrigerator and took out the small can wrapped in layers of plastic wrap and plastic bags in an effort to contain the smell. It was actually successful and there wasn't even a hint of nauseating fish smell until I'd gone through several layers of plastic.

I put a dab of the pink mush in his bowl and he was on it before I picked up the can. He was already finished and off for a nap by the time I did all the rewrapping.

I ended the process by washing my hands with lemon soap, taking away even a hint of the stench, and finally headed out the door. I once again thought how lucky I was to be located so close to Vista Del Mar, both because the rustic atmosphere spilled across to my place and because it made it so quick and easy to get there, which came in handy during the retreats.

I took a deep breath of the brisk moist air and felt it energize me. Already I felt better about the prospects of Madeleine's retreat, as I was coming to think of it. It was one step at a time.

As I'd expected, the Lodge was mostly empty. There were a few people who had come in after breakfast and were using the pay phones in the vintage booths in the front, or checking the message board back near the gift shop.

Even for the people who chose Vista Del Mar because it was completely unplugged, there was always some adjustment. Most people didn't even know how to use a pay phone anymore, and reading a message that had been taken for them by the staff and stuck on a cork board was a lot different than dealing with a text.

I was relieved to see that Cloris was alone behind the registration desk, and when I scanned the whole space, there was no sign of Kevin St. John. I'd have to deal with him eventually, but it would be so much easier if the arrangements were already in place.

I had been dealing with Cloris since the time she'd worked in the kitchen. She'd always made sure there were refreshments for my retreat group and gotten me extras from the kitchen when I ate there. She was studying hospitality at the local community college and had been more than willing to fill in anywhere when it was needed. She had been rewarded by getting the position of assistant manager. Though the promotion hadn't come from Kevin St. John. It was more in spite of him and had come by way of the Delacorte family with a little help from me. I'd only ever known her as Cloris; like Cher, she seemed to go by one name. It was only when she became assistant manager that I saw the name on her badge said Cloris Dunphy. The rest of her life was a mystery.

"Ms. Delacorte really dropped a big one in your lap," Cloris said once I'd explained the situation. Her dark hair was pulled into an efficient-looking low bun and she wore the uniform blue blazer with her name tag with pride. It was a big change from the wild blue hair and jeans she'd worn when her uniform was a white kitchen smock. The title hadn't gone to her head and she still helped out anywhere that was needed, even in housekeeping.

"The guest rooms are no problem. You can have the first floor of the Sand and Sea building. I'd say we'd try to block out the rooms on the second floor, but we already have a reservation for one of the rooms. There's a note that it's for a repeat guest and they were specific about that room." The meeting room I always used was available and we agreed on a parlor in the Gulls building for the teas. "As for the program," she said with a pleased look. "I think I have just what you need." She stepped back from the counter and pulled out a folder.

"I tried to show it to Mr. St. John, but he wouldn't even look at it." She opened it and started to pull out pages. "It's the final project from last semester's class on creating extra business. We were supposed to create a plan for an event we could host." Her smile broadened. "With all these true crime podcasts and TV shows, people seemed to have become enamored with playing detective. I created the scenario for just the sort of thing you're talking about. I called it *Murder at the Seaside Resort*."

She had the script with her and showed it to me. It was just as Frank had suggested with the guests as the detectives and hotel staff playing the parts of the victim and such. I told her I was calling the weekend *A Murderous Yarn* and she was fine with the change. Just then Kevin St. John came into the building. He was dressed as always in a dark suit that looked more like it belonged on a funeral director than the manager of the rustic hotel and conference center. He gave

Cloris a nod and me a pursed lip look of annoyance.

"Let him give us dirty looks," I said. "Just wait until he finds out that there's a part for him. He can't refuse or interfere with the retreat since Madeleine is the one who has requested it."

I expected Cloris to say something in agreement, but she was strangely silent, and when I looked at her face it seemed clouded with worry.

"Is something wrong?" I asked. I realized I'd mis-phrased the question. There was no doubt something was wrong—what I really wanted to know was what it was. My concern got tabled as the manager approached us. He was eyeing the counter and the papers on it.

"Should I know about this?" he asked, looking from one of us to the other. I wasn't so sure if I wanted to tell him about it yet, but Cloris went right into it.

"We were setting things up for Casey's next retreat." She went into describing that it was going to be different than the ones I'd put on and would be using her final project. I watched him as he listened, getting more irritated by the moment as he heard about a staged murder and Vista Del Mar employees playing parts. He was waiting for a break to interrupt and no doubt put the kibosh on the whole thing. As she got to the end of it she looked at me to add the finish.

"I can't wait to tell Madeleine Delacorte about all the arrangements," I said, playing innocent. "This was all her idea and she's going to have an integral part in the whole event."

It was like sticking a pin in a balloon as his expression deflated and he realized like it or not, he was going to have to go along with it and worse, even be a part of it.

"I can't discuss it now," he said in a dismissive tone, trying to save himself. "I have guests to attend to." He walked over to a couple who had just walked in.

"This is going to be fun," I said, turning to Cloris, but she'd gotten the worried look again. This time I thought before I spoke and asked her specifically what was wrong.

"I think Mr. St. John is looking for a way to get rid of me," she said. "It wasn't his idea to make me assistant manager and he resents that I have the job."

I tried to reassure her that he couldn't do that. "You're so good at what you do, always doing more than you have to. And everybody likes you. How could he possibly justify firing you?"

"He could find a way to discredit me and get the Delacortes to agree with him."

"They're not going to change their minds about you. Certainly not when I tell Madeleine how you're turning her idea into a reality." Cloris seemed a little more hopeful and thanked me profusely. "And now let's get back to planning the mystery weekend."

She urged me to take her folder and look everything over and then we could make specific plans and decide who would play what character. I left feeling a huge sense of relief. I should have known that Cloris would come up with something. Now that I was confident there was a plan, I ran the ads and sent out the emails. Madeleine was right that October with the hint of Halloween spookiness was the perfect time for the retreat. The response was quick and all the spots were taken in a few days, and I even had a waiting list.

I kept Madeleine in the loop and she was happy with everything I told her, but seemed to want to stay on the sidelines. That worked for me.

With all the concern about the mystery, I couldn't forget about the yarn. They were yarn retreats after all. I waited until I had all the registration forms filled out so I had an idea who I was going to be dealing with. Already I knew this retreat was going to be different. There were two couples, a single man, two single women, a mother and daughter and finally Madeleine. I brought the list and all the materials to show Crystal Smith.

We'd agreed to meet at Cadbury Yarn. Gwen Selwyn had opened the store when Crystal was a toddler and it had always been part of her life. She'd even shown me the pair of plastic knitting needles she'd used to make her first scarf.

The store was housed in a bungalow on a sloping side street in the main part of town. A breeze kept the rainbow wind sock twirling as I crossed the small porch and went inside. As usual Crystal was a rainbow of colors. She had a yellow, purple and green T-shirt showing under the black one she wore on top. I didn't look at her feet, but I knew her bright-colored socks didn't match. It was deliberate on her part. As were the unmatched earrings. Her black hair was just long enough so it curled into corkscrews. I felt so dull in comparison in my ordinary jeans and a black sweatshirt.

She took me into a back room that probably had been a bedroom but was now used as an office.

She was about my age, but at a very different place in her life. She was divorced with two kids. Her ex was a self-proclaimed rock god who had left Crystal for a younger version of her. Being married with kids wasn't his thing, nor was a regular life that required him to take out the trash or change a lightbulb. Crystal and her kids had come back to Cadbury and moved in with her mother.

I was partly responsible for their lives being shaken up. I hadn't meant to cause any problems, but by chance had found out that Gwen was the love child of the Delacorte sisters' late brother Edmund.

Edmund had been the one to buy Vista Del Mar after the camp had been abandoned and it was a rundown cheap resort. He had a passion for the place and had refurbished the buildings and protected the grounds and sand dunes. He had specifically left it to his heirs, but his only son had preceded him in death, so when he died, Vista Del Mar went to the sisters.

Gwen would have left things as they were except for her grandson Cory. He was already working at Vista Del Mar part-time and had a passion for the place that turned out to be genetic. I wasn't privy to whatever arrangement they made other than the sisters acknowledged Gwen and her family were relatives and had some part in Vista Del Mar.

"You called me your yarn craft consultant. It sounds a little corporate," Crystal said with a laugh, gesturing toward her outfit. I always admired how she pulled off wearing a lot of eye makeup. I'd tried to emulate it more than once and let's just say the reaction I got was laughter. Somehow she pulled off the whole look without looking silly.

She continued to laugh as she read over the pages describing the weekend. "This sounds like so much fun. How did you ever get Kevin St. John to agree to let you do it and play a part in it?"

"Four words," I said. "Madeleine asked for it."

Crystal raised her eyebrows in amusement. "I wish I could have been there when you talked to him. He probably got all flustered because he knew you had the upper hand."

"I should have thought of bringing you. Then he really would have had to contain his fuss."

"Except that I like to keep a low profile about being a Delacorte. I wonder if Kevin even remembers that Madeleine and Cora are my great-aunts." Crystal shook her head and laughed at the thought. It was hard to picture her with her wild outfits as being related to the very proper Delacorte sisters.

"Madeleine is going to be Mrs. Maple," Crystal said with another laugh. "She's certainly coming out of her shell after all these years. First it was wearing all that denim, unlike Cora with her Chanel suits, and now she wants to play at being a detective." She turned to me. "I hope you realize you're going to have to steer her in the right direction." Despite that Crystal seemed to want to stay separate from the Delacorte family, she and Madeleine liked each other.

I nodded, knowing that I had to make sure that the weekend was a success for Madeleine more than even my paying guests.

While we were talking, Crystal had picked up a pair of circular needles and was working on a pair of socks. She was able to work with only an occasional look at her work. I envied how yarn craft was second nature to her. I'd improved with each retreat I'd put on, but I still had to pay close attention to what I was doing. And knit two socks at once—no way.

We finally got down to business, discussing what sort of project we'd have the group do. In my other yarn retreats, the guests always brought some of their own projects to work on along with whatever we came up with. I didn't know how it would be with this group.

"Since there are going to be a number of men and all of their skill levels are questionable, I think we should go with something unisex and easy. I suppose we could do a scarf," she said.

"It seems kind of dull," I said.

"I have another idea. What about hand warmers?" she offered. She rummaged around in a bin and pulled out something that looked like a tube made in shades of brown and gave it to me to try on. It seemed quite appealing as I held out my hand and checked it out as I wiggled my fingers.

"You think guys would be happy with it?" I said.

"Everybody gets cold hands. You can ask Dane. Football players wear them," she said as she pulled out another one and handed it to me. I put it on my other hand and then held them close together, comparing the two knitted pieces. The one on my right hand started out in a golden tan and morphed into more of a tree bark brown. The one on my left began in a grayish beige and then a mushroom brown.

"I know they don't exactly match. That's why I love them," she said. "I promise they are made from the same skein of yarn." She got up and went to the cubbies filled with their stock and returned holding a skein of yarn that looked like a small brown cake. When she showed me the top of it, there were stripes of different shades of beige and brown.

I already knew that it was called self-striping yarn because it made stripes as you knitted or crocheted with it. It worked fine with a scarf or hat, but the hand warmers started in different places in the color scheme, so they blended, but weren't a mirror image. It made sense that she would like the concept, I thought, noticing that her earrings, as usual, didn't match. "I think it's a fun idea, but I'm not so sure how this group would handle it. All I really know about them is that they like mysteries."

"I suppose you're right," she said, sounding disappointed.

I took a moment to think about it and came up with a solution. "The obvious answer is we offer the cakes of self-striping yarn, and a selection of solid colors for the more traditional people in the group."

"I like it," she said with a pleased smile. "I'll bring samples of them made both ways." With that, she picked up the circular needles and started back working on the socks. "So, what's up with you and Dane?"

I put up my hands in a hopeless manner and we went from talking about the retreat to girl talk. She was understanding about my wanting to stay independent and then she told me that she'd been seeing someone on the QT.

"I don't know how you can manage that here," I said, thinking how Dane thought people driving by might see him hug me.

"It's not here," she said. "He's a singer-songwriter and he plays at a bar in Monterey."

"A musician?" I said, thinking of what she'd already been through with one.

"It's just like a hobby. He has a day job working for the city." She smiled a little sheepishly. "I admit it, I have a weakness for musicians, but he's not like Rixx. He's actually a grown-up and he was more than happy to get on a ladder and help with the store lightbulbs. His name is Robert." I had never said anything to her about it, but I thought her rock god ex calling himself Rixx was totally pretentious.

We both agreed that it was nice to have each other to talk to. I asked her if she knew anything about Cloris.

"Not beyond that she seems to always be at Vista Del Mar and Cory says nice things about her.

"She's always done so much to help me with the retreats, and when she worked in the kitchen, she knew just what I liked and would make up a plate for me. And here, I know nothing about her life outside of Vista Del Mar. When this retreat is all done, I think we should have a girls' night. You, Lucinda, Cloris and me."

"Absolutely, but if Madeleine finds out, she's going to want to come."

"Sure, why not." I looked at the two socks on the circular needles that were identical twins. "What gives? Are you actually going to have a pair of socks that match?"

"Never," Crystal said as she stuck out her feet and showed off that she was wearing a shocking pink sock and a black one with pink polka dots. "These are for my daughter, who finds the way I dress totally embarrassing."

Chapter 4

I had kept Madeleine up to date as the plans came together for the retreat and had invited her to the dress rehearsal I'd put together for the Wednesday evening before everyone arrived. She declined and made the excuse that it might give Mrs. Maple inside information and she wanted to be on the same level as the rest of the group.

I had been surprised when she requested a guest room in the same building with the same accommodations as everyone else rather than going home to her fabulous Victorian house with a view of the whole town. I even asked if she didn't want one of the special rooms, but she insisted she wanted to seem like one of the retreaters. What could I do but arrange for it?

The dress rehearsal was actually pretty casual and everyone was to meet in the Lodge. Most of them were going to wear what they did normally for work, but I'd gotten costumes for a few of the people. They already knew their parts and had a script with plenty of room for improv to use when they were questioned by the retreat group. This was really just a last chance to go over it again.

I got there early and parked the bin packed with everything next to the seating around the huge stone fireplace. Wednesday was the slowest day of the week at the hotel. People who had been there for a long weekend had gone and people coming for an extended weekend like my group usually came on Thursday.

Cloris was standing outside the counter and I went to talk to her about rounding everyone up, and to find out about the other guests who were going to be at Vista Del Mar that weekend.

"We have them," she said discreetly, indicating a group wearing red shirts with some writing on them who had taken up the pool table and the one for table tennis. There were ten people, mostly men, and they seemed to be giving the games their all. Someone scored and they let out a raucous cheer that echoed through the room. "Sorry," she said, noticing that I'd put my hand over my ear to dull the sound. "I have orders to let them do whatever they want. They're a business group who comes here periodically and Mr. St. John wants to make sure they keep coming. They spend a lot in the café and pay for extras like having us arrange excursions."

"So, you're saying they're supposed to get extra consideration," I said and she nodded.

"And they know it. They have a sense of entitlement. I hope they don't interfere with your group." She looked at me. "The rest of the guests are the usual families, along with some couples and singles looking to get away from it all for a few days. We have a few people who have been here all week."

"Hopefully there won't be any problems," I said. In addition to providing the scenario, Cloris had a part in it. She was basically playing herself and using her uniform as her costume. There was no need to go over what she was supposed to do because other than a little tweaking we'd done, we were using what she'd created.

"Where is Ms. Delacorte?" Kevin St. John said, coming from the back office area. As soon as I mentioned she wasn't coming, he turned surly. "I don't need a dress rehearsal. You've already told me about my part as the manager of a hotel. I don't need a costume. I know what I'm supposed to say."

Cloris stepped in and smoothed things over. "Since you are the one in charge, you need to know what everybody else is doing." Being reminded that he was the boss seemed to work and he became more agreeable. I wondered if one of her classes in hospitality at the community college was devoted to dealing with difficult people. If so, she must have aced it.

Thankfully, he was the only one who objected to our meeting. But then it was no surprise really. He was always looking for a way to give me a hard time with my retreats, annoyed that he couldn't get rid of me. I wasn't the only one the manager was unhappy with. I saw the way his lips pursed when his gaze stopped on Cory Smith, who had just come in.

It was totally ridiculous. Crystal's son loved Vista Del Mar, and despite the fact that technically he was one of the owners, he never acted like it. He probably would have made the same suggestions for things like walkie-talkies if he'd just been a high school kid working there part-time.

He had a lanky build where his arms and legs seemed too long for his body and the kind of attitude that took everything in stride. His part in our drama was "the porter," and he was excited to be one of the suspects.

"This is going to be fun," Cory said as I handed him his costume, which was just a vest with some silver buttons and a bow tie. He wanted to be sure that he had it right and that it was okay to improvise when the group questioned him.

Lucinda came into the area just as Cory was trying on the vest. Technically, she didn't have to be part of our ensemble, but she was not only my boss at the restaurant but also a friend who had frequently attended my retreats. And the Blue Door was catering the extra food service that Madeleine had requested. The Sea Foam dining hall offered meals for all the guests, but the menu was more like camp food than haute cuisine. The best they could offer for the reception we had planned was cheese and crackers, along with chips and dips. I couldn't even imagine what they would have come up with for a cream tea.

As always, Lucinda was perfectly put together in a Ralph Loren denim dress and I hoped she wouldn't mind wearing the black uniform with the white apron and headdress.

We had kept to leaving her husband out of it. Not only did he need to handle the restaurant while she was gone, but with his bordering on OCD, I could only imagine how he would handle playing one of the parts, particularly since we weren't being exact about the time period *A Murderous Yarn* was supposed to take place. We were going more for the illusion of a past time than anything too authentic, which would drive him crazy.

"Aren't we missing someone?" Cloris said, glancing around.

"I'm here," Sammy said, rushing up. "The victim has arrived." The tall man with the teddy bear build said it a little too loudly and I shushed him. "Sorry, Case." He was the only one who called me Case, which barely seemed to count as a nickname. I saw the soulful look in his dark eyes and looked away. His feelings were too transparent and made me uncomfortable.

"We needed someone who could disappear after," I explained to the group. "How would it look if the victim was back pushing a housekeeper cart after the murder?"

Sammy Glickner was not an employee of the hotel, but since he occasionally did close-up magic in the dining hall, I'd asked him to be part of the charade. He was really Dr. Sammy Glickner, a urologist and my ex-boyfriend. He insisted that he hadn't followed me to Cadbury with any hopes of us getting back together, but rather it was a place where he could practice medicine and do his magic away from the judgmental stares of his family.

We were quite a pair, both well into our thirties and still concerned about parental approval. My mother continued to hang on to the hope that somehow Sammy and I would end up together. Sammy was a good guy and I cared about him, but there was just no chemistry. No heat. No magic in his kiss. It wasn't one of those things I could will either. There was no problem in that department with Dane. I felt my cheeks flush as I remembered our last breakfast rendezvous.

Sammy was playing an international man of mystery who did magic tricks. There was a little extra drama thrown in, like he knew secrets about a bunch of people and had dealings with a gangster called El Bosso. Sammy enthusiastically went over the encounters he was supposed to have before he turned up dead.

He wowed the group with a few card tricks and made sure it was okay to stray from the script. I assured him anything extra would be appreciated. He took my arm and leaned in close. "You know I'd do anything for you. I bet not everyone you know would say that." His gaze went around the area as if he was looking to point out that a a specific someone wasn't there. I knew he meant Dane. Although Sammy had not said anything directly, I knew he knew there had been a step up in my relationship with Dane, and he was upset by it.

I was just glad that after Sammy's emergency stay in my guesthouse, he'd moved back to the apartment that had been added on to the bed-and-breakfast. I'd been happy to help him out when there'd been a plumbing disaster at his place, but it was a little too close for comfort.

Bob, one of the baristas in the café, joined the group. He was playing a barista. His uniform was another vest with a name tag. His bland looks and relaxed manner generally kept him in the background. He was enthused about being in the action for a change

"Sorry if I'm late," a woman in a housekeeper's pale blue dress said as she came up to me. "There was a last-minute switch. Jane can't do it, so I'm standing in for her. She already told me what I'm supposed to say."

I thanked her for taking Jane's place but said it was too late to make up a new name tag. "I hope this is okay," I said and handed her the pin that said Jane.

Cloris handed me the bag of clues we were going to leave for my group. I looked through it and took out a coaster from the café with a note on it. There was a paper cup with brownish lipstick on the rim. Cloris smiled and pointed out it was same shade she was wearing. In addition, there was a receipt with a time stamp, a footprint on a sheet of paper, a silver button, and a king of spades playing card with something written on it.

I had just reminded everyone what time to be there the next day to greet the arrivals when a woman threaded through the group and went into the arrangement of couches and chairs around the fireplace.

She was dressed in sweats and a baseball cap that threw a shadow over her face. What little I could see of it seemed red, and I thought she must not have realized that even with the perpetual cloudy skies it was possible to get a sunburn. She seemed uncertain about taking a seat and Kevin St. John put on his cloying manager smile and went to her side.

"Make yourself comfortable," he said. "This crowd is just leaving and you'll have peace to read." He gestured to the book in her hand. She seemed about to take one of the mission-style chairs when a man came into the seating area. He gave us all a hard look and I thought Kevin was going to give him the same speech, but the woman spoke first, surprising all of us with her sharp tone.

"I know what you're doing," she said. "Get away from me and leave me alone."

I looked at the man to see his reaction. It was as though he willed himself to smile at her before he turned to us. "I was just trying to be friendly."

He was ordinary-looking in a pair of beige cargo pants and a black fleece vest, and frankly didn't seem like someone on the prowl. As he backed away, one of the guys in the red shirts caught up with him. Ever curious, I leaned in to hear their conversation.

"Hey pal, good to see you." The man in the red shirt shot a glance back at the woman in the baseball cap. "You must get a lot of that. Let me buy you a beer." He pointed at the open door to the café. As they walked away, I saw the man in the fleece vest look back in our direction, though his gaze settled on the woman in the baseball cap.

My natural nosiness clicked in and I wondered what the story was, but Kevin St. John hustled us all out into the main part of the room. He took over, dismissing the group before he gave me a look. "She's not one of your retreaters and not your concern. In other words, mind your own business."

Chapter 5

Sammy had wanted to hang out and talk over an idea he had about something he wanted to add to his magic act. He was doing more than close-up magic now and had been hired to do some shows at the posh resorts in nearby Pebble Beach. I'd been acting as his assistant temporarily until he found someone permanent, which was beginning to seem like never. He always said I was the only one who *got him.* I hated to admit it, but it was probably true. Sammy was a good guy and I cared about him, just not in the way he wanted. But I had a lot on my mind and my night was far from over and I put him off until after the retreat.

I still had dessert and muffin baking to do, along with extras for the afternoon tea Madeleine had requested. I stopped home to pick up the supplies and hoped to keep it to a quick in and out. But there was no getting past Julius. He was perched on the kitchen counter and had a perfect view of the back door. He jumped down as soon as I came in and did a brief figure eight around my ankles and then sprinted across the floor. When the black cat reached the basic white refrigerator, he let out a plaintive meow in case I hadn't gotten the hint that it was time for a snack.

He was my first animal companion and I was sympathetic since it seemed that he'd been abandoned. Probably too sympathetic. In my desire to please him, I'd bought a selection of canned cat food. You'd think that since he'd been abandoned, any food from a can would please him, but Julius dismissed the tuna and meat that smelled like prime rib and settled on the mackerel delight. I suppose to him part of the "delight" was the strong smell.

He let out another meow to hint that I wasn't moving fast enough. "You win," I said, making my way to the refrigerator. And then began the layers of unwrapping. I'd learned to not breathe through my nose during the whole process.

It seemed like a big fuss for the small dab of pinkish fish I put in his bowl, but I'd discovered the hard way that if he was given too much at one time, he would throw it up. The smell was even worse the second time around. The dab pleased him and there were no aftereffects, which pleased me.

It was late when I got to the Blue Door and I had to use my key to get in. As I turned on the lights, I saw that the main dining area was already set up for the next day's lunch. A line of empty cake plates covered with glass domes sat on the counter by the door, waiting for my creations. It took two trips to bring in all of my supplies since in addition to the desserts for the Blue Door and muffins for my other customers, I was making things for the afternoon tea reception we were putting on the first afternoon. I had a lot of worries about being able to pull off the murder game and satisfy Madeleine and the paying guests, but I felt confident about my baking.

The soft jazz in the background soothed my mood and I started making the batter for the pound cakes. I had chosen them because they could be served in a variety of different ways. I made an extra one for the retreat group's afternoon tea. Once they were in the oven, I got lost in the smell of sweet things baking and in a rhythm of mashing bananas for the muffins. The cakes were cooling on wire racks and I'd just put the pans of muffins in the oven when I heard a rap on the glass portion of the front door. Dane had actually given me advance warning that he was coming by so I went to the door with no worries it was an intruder.

"I heard about the rehearsal. I'm sure Sammy was there," he said and I nodded. He knew all about my past relationship with Sammy—emphasis on the past, as in over with—and despite me explaining numerous times that I viewed Sammy only as a good friend, there was always an edge in Dane's voice when he talked about him. It didn't help that I was still his assistant for the magic act. "I might not be able to play a part in the mystery scenario, but I can offer you some moral support," Dane said, putting his arm over my shoulder. It jostled the radio hooked to his shoulder and it pulled loose. As he went to reposition it, he began with his pep talk, reminding me I had put on a lot of retreats with plenty of difficult people.

"I appreciate the support, but I've never done one like this where there's a murder," I said.

He tilted his head and looked at me. "You mean not one that was planned."

I groaned. "At least this one isn't real." He went on to reassure me that Madeleine was probably not nearly as hard to please as I imagined. He was interrupted by a sharp knock on the door.

Once he understood that I wasn't expecting anyone, he offered to handle whoever was there, but I felt it was my responsibility. In the end, we both went to the door.

We peered through the glass portion of the door in unison and I heard Dane groan as he made out the bulldog face of Lieutenant Borgnine.

"Okay you caught me," Dane said, putting his hands up in capitulation as his superior came inside. "But I'm on a break so there is no dereliction of duty."

"Relax, Mangano," the lieutenant said. "Everybody knows you hang out with your girlfriend. I'm here to talk to her." He seemed to have a permanent gruff expression and generally seemed annoyed with me. It wasn't good when some amateur bested you at solving crimes. I tensed up, wondering what was wrong now.

"I heard you're planning some kind of fake murder party at Vista Del Mar," he said. He shook his head decisively. "You should have consulted with me. I'm going to have to shut it down. We can't have people thinking that murder is an amusement in Cadbury." Just then I heard the timer go off and excused myself to go to the kitchen. They both followed me. The air smelled heavenly of banana muffins. I had long given up on cutesy names since the town council made a fuss when I called my muffins names like Plain Janes and Raisin to Be. I hadn't realized their obsession with making everything authentic. The seaside town attracted tourists from around the world, but there were no ye olde anything shops or anything that seemed to cater to the visitors.

"You're kidding. Shut it down?" I said, almost in a shriek. "But it starts tomorrow." I glanced at my watch and saw that it was after midnight. "I mean today. My people are probably all packed and ready to go."

I could hear the lieutenant sniffing the air. He might not be a fan of my detective work but he loved the muffins. I pulled the pans out of the vertical oven and set them out on the counter to cool. The delicious fragrance was even stronger. "Give them a minute to cool and then help yourself," I said to the older cop, knowing it would soften him up.

He looked at me. "I know what you're doing. You're trying to bribe me with baked goods. I probably should refuse the offer." He let out his breath before giving the muffins another once-over. "They're banana, aren't they?" He looked at them again. "Mrs. Borgnine is always after me to eat more fruit. How much of a bribe can a muffin be. It's not like you're offering an envelope full of cash."

I plucked one of the muffins out and put it on a plate for him. He cut it in pieces, and even as the steam was still coming off it popped one in his mouth. His pleased expression said it all. He looked at Dane. "A bribe is only a bribe if it works. It's not going to change my mind about this event you want to put on. It's a bad idea. I won't have your turning a homicide into an amusement. Why can't you stick with your yarn stuff?"

"It wasn't my idea," I said. "I'm doing it at the request of Madeleine Delacorte." The lieutenant was reaching for another piece of muffin but dropped it.

"Oh," he said as he shook his head in understanding. She and Cora were treated with reverence since they owned so much property in the town in addition to Vista Del Mar and were benefactors to all the charities. He knew he was beat. "I wish Kevin St. John had told me that."

"If you'd like we could include you as a character. The local cop who helps with the game," I said and he gave me a withering look.

"No, thank you." He turned to Dane. "And you better not either." He retrieved the muffin piece he'd dropped on the plate and ate it with a sigh. "I suppose it's okay, as long as there are no actual weapons, and nobody better really turn up dead."

"Of course not," I said with a laugh. Even though the tagline for the theme was *the hotel where everyone who checks in doesn't check out.*

Chapter 6

I awoke with the jitters, and that was before I'd even had coffee. No more time to prep or work out any problems. My people would be arriving in a few hours. Julius didn't seem concerned and demanded his first taste of the day of stink fish as soon as I got in the kitchen. I couldn't sit still to drink a whole cup of coffee and after a few sips went to get dressed.

Our weekend was supposed to be set in the past, but we never settled on an exact decade. The instructions told our group to dress reminiscent of another time. I realized now that we should have been a little more specific. Somebody could show up in a toga.

Madeleine's Mrs. Maple suits made me think of 1940s or '50s fashion. I didn't have an old wardrobe to choose from, so I looked to old movies to get ideas. I certainly wasn't going to wear a slinky evening gown or a suit with a weird fur stole slung around my neck like Myrna Loy did in the Thin Man movies. Did they really wear fashion items that had the animal's head and feet still on them? Oh, yuck. I decided to go for more of a Katherine Hepburn look because I liked it better and I actually owned several pairs of loose-fitting trousers and a couple of white collared shirts. I had laid everything out in advance so I wouldn't be in a panic thrashing around the closet looking for something to wear.

I didn't have the sharp jaw of the actress, but with my hair loose when I looked in the mirror, I did have a yesterday sort of look and it was comfortable besides. I kept to a comfortable level of makeup, which meant not much. Though I admired Crystal's smudgy eyes, it wasn't something I could pull off. Instead of sultry, I looked silly.

The phone rang when I was looking through my aunt's stash of knitted and crocheted accessories. I hesitated for a moment, but only for a moment before I decided to let it go to voicemail. By the time of the morning, I knew it was my mother. It was two hours later in Chicago, which she never seemed to get straight despite being a cardiologist. Actually, I'm sure she knew what time it was but was too impatient to wait any longer to call. To say that she was upset with my life choices was an understatement. Her calls usually ended with some reminder that at my age she had already been a wife, mother and doctor. There was a silence after that, which was her way of saying *and what are you?*

It was useless to explain that we were different sort of people. I knew she was trying to be supportive with her offers of cooking school in Paris or a detective academy in Los Angeles. She was hung up on certificates. In all fairness, I did keep those two offers in the back of my mind. But certainly not this weekend. I hadn't told her anything about this retreat and I knew she wouldn't approve.

When the ringing stopped, I went back to going through the stash. I always picked one of her creations and added it to my outfit. It was meant to be in remembrance of Aunt Joan and also with the hope it might bring her spirit around to help me pull this weekend off. Nothing had been said, but I wasn't sure what Madeleine would do if her "job" as being Mrs. Maple didn't live up to her expectations. But it couldn't be good.

The crocheted lion sat on the desk and seemed to be watching me as I plucked out a tan scarf that blended with the brown tweed pants. The added bonus was it would add a little warmth since I was wearing a cotton shirt instead of the warm turtleneck sweater I usually wore for retreats. I replaced my usual fleece jacket with a heavy sweater. I did cheat when it came to shoes and stuck with sneakers, though they were largely hidden under the cuffs of the tweed pants.

I moved on to the guesthouse, where I had the tote bags ready to take across the street. The blood red ones with *Yarn2Go* emblazoned on the front seemed wrong for this group and I'd stuck to natural-colored ones. I always stocked them with some luxury items like small sizes of fancy toiletries, a lavender sachet to put under their pillow to add a nice scent and act as a natural sleep aid. There was always chocolate, too. I'd added small bags of bridge mix this time. Then there were the papers. On top of information about Vista Del Mar and their schedule of activities, I had created a packet with everything about the mystery. I had a few pages with the story line and characters along with a sealed envelope with copies of the clues only to be opened after the victim's demise.

Added to my concerns was Madeleine's insistence on staying at Vista Del Mar with the others. Despite being an owner, I wasn't sure she realized how sparse the accommodations were. She was used to a posh bedroom in a Victorian house overlooking Monterey Bay. How was she going to feel staying in a room that had more of a feeling of a camp than a luxurious hotel?

I could feel the tension rising as I packed all the tote bags and my clipboard and such into a bin on wheels. I was already second-guessing myself, wondering if it was a mistake not to have included everything for the yarn project, but Crystal thought it was better to keep everything for the hand warmers separate.

It was midday as I wheeled the bin down the driveway toward the Lodge, though you couldn't tell by the sky. The sun was hidden somewhere above the layer of white. After growing up in Chicago, where there was a joke about if you didn't like the weather, wait five minutes, it got a little monotonous here. The temperature was mostly in the sixties and if the sun came out, it wasn't for long. It was a treat when I could actually see my shadow.

I went directly to the Lodge. There was a din of conversations and for the first time it sunk in that I was going to have to deal with my group in the midst of all these others. Madeleine had stayed out of the planning except for a few "suggestions." The biggest one was that she thought we should greet the arriving retreaters the way they did guests in the *Downton Abbey* TV show. They would have a line of the staff and members of the family outside as someone arrived.

We were going to have the line assembled across the front of the Lodge in full view of the people reading in the seating area or shooting pool in the back of the room. There was no time to make any changes now, so I pulled the bin into the café to leave it before I checked on the setup. Madeleine was sitting at a table and Cloris was setting down a cup of something for her. As soon as Madeleine saw me, she popped out of the chair.

"Mrs. Maple reporting for duty," she said with an animated smile. "I was so excited, I could barely sleep. My idea is coming to life." She seemed dazzled by the concept and blissfully unaware of the work done by others—mostly me—to make it happen. The main thing she had contributed was clout. It was only by telling everyone that she was behind the murder mystery retreat that they agreed to it.

She was dressed in another tweed suit that made her look shapeless and formidable. When she'd worn all the denim, it had shaved years off of her appearance. The suit had put them all back on and then some. Cloris grabbed the large suitcase that was sitting next to the table and wheeled it out, explaining she'd put it in the area set aside for the others.

I appreciated all the help, but the arrival of my retreaters was always nerve-wracking. It was a group of strangers that I had to get to know and try to please all weekend. And that was when it was just a weekend devoted to yarn craft. This time there was so much more to deal with, along with being Madeleine's sidekick.

Madeleine left her drink and followed me back into the main room. Cloris was standing in front of the registration counter with a knot of people. The players were all assuming their characters, seeming nervous and excited at the same time. I knew the feeling. As she began to arrange them into a line, Kevin St. John came out from the back area. He had a resistant expression until he saw Madeleine and then he went to reserved enthusiasm.

A crowd of anybody at the front would have attracted attention, but an actual reception line with some people in costumes had everyone in the cavernous room staring at us.

"Maybe you should let everyone know about our game," I said to Kevin St. John as he took the first position in the line.

"You should have brought that up sooner. I didn't realize what a spectacle this retreat was going to be," he sputtered in annoyance.

"What about that group in the red shirts? I hope they aren't going to interfere with us," I said.

"They should be no concern of yours. They're from Glucon Insurance and come here to work on their skills."

I left him and went down the line to do a final inspection. Cloris was next to the manager and looked trim in her blue blazer. Lucinda did a mock bow to me, showing off her black uniform and peaked white hat as she took the next spot. "I was kind of hoping I'd get to wear one of Cora's Chanel suits," she said with a good-natured smile to let me know she was joking. Even though I'm sure with her love of designer clothes there was some truth in it. Bob the barista appeared a little sheepish as he stopped next to Lucinda. He was used to being a fixture in the café and not on display like this.

"Where do you want me?" Cory said. The teenager was so unassuming that no one would ever guess that he was really part of the Delacorte family. I pointed and he slipped in next to Bob and seemed to be enjoying being a part of the whole escapade. I saw Crystal hanging off in the corner watching. Even though she was technically staff since she was in charge of the yarn craft, she'd wanted to stay out of the mystery portion and the greeting committee. Last was the stand-in for Jane the housekeeper.

And we were ready to begin.

Chapter 7

I'd been so concerned about arranging the reception line I hadn't been paying attention to anything else. Now I saw that a group of people had been gathering around us and I assumed they were the retreaters. I asked them to arrange themselves in a line before I took the spot at the head of the greeters. Taking a deep breath, I held my clipboard at the ready and waved the first person toward me.

"Mary Smith," she said, glancing down at my list. She was short with a roundish shape and white hair cut in a precise blunt cut.

"It's just you?" I asked as I glanced down the list.

"Yes, just me," she said in a sharp tone. "Is that a problem?" I realized she had taken what I said wrong and I rushed to try to explain without making it worse.

"Being here on your own is fine," I said. "All the more space in the room for you," I said brightly. "I only asked because sometimes people register separately but are traveling together."

She seemed okay with the explanation and looked at my outfit. "The information I got said to dress in a nostalgic style." She pointed to her black slacks and royal blue untucked shirt with a long black sweater. "Is this acceptable?"

"It was just a suggestion," I said. "There are no rules. We were just hoping to set a mood." I couldn't tell by her expression how she felt about what I'd said. I glanced down at her name and saw that I'd put a question mark next to it. I thumbed through the sheets underneath until I came to a printout of her registration form. She had left the occupation slot blank. "Did you want to list your profession?" I asked.

"I thought that was a little intrusive," she said. "What difference should it make what I do?" I was surprised by her reaction. I'd put it in the form more out of curiosity than any real need.

"I'll just leave it blank," I said with a pleasant smile. "You'll be a woman of mystery." I meant the comment in a light way and expected a smile in response, but there wasn't a hint of curve in her lips.

Madeleine had positioned herself nearby on her own and introduced herself.

"I'm Mrs. Maple," she said. "I'm the house detective." She added a smile. "Just in case something happens."

Mary Smith didn't seem to know quite what to make of Madeleine. I wasn't exactly sure what to make of her either. It seemed that Madeleine had taken it upon herself to up her part to house detective. I pointed to the greeting committee and urged Mary to work her way down. "And then what?" she asked in a sharp tone. I felt my stomach clench. I'd done enough retreats to recognize when someone was going to be a problem. We'd barely met and already I knew that she was hiding something and going to be trouble. Even though Jane, as the last in the line, had been instructed to tell them to leave their suitcase and go into the café, I told Mary directly. She wanted to know what was going to happen after that.

"We'll all have a drink and get to know each other a little and you'll get your room key, tote bag with goodies and more," I said in a friendly voice. I couldn't tell if she liked what she heard or not, but I was glad when she moved on and started working her way down the line.

A man came up to me next and gave me his name, but I'd already figured he probably wasn't one of our people by his attire. He was wearing cargo shorts, hiking sandals and a floppy hat. He was disappointed when I explained about the mystery weekend.

"I wish I'd known," he said. "I love a good murder. Is it too late to sign up?" I could tell that Kevin St. John was listening as I broke it gently to the man that it was part of a yarn craft retreat and that we had a full house. He glanced at the row of greeters and with a sad shrug walked away.

A couple moved up once he was gone. I guessed they were in their late thirties and seemed very stylish. He was in khakis and a polo shirt with a sweater tied around his shoulders. I'd been hanging around Lucinda enough to recognize that her taupe chino pants and herringbone blazer with suede patches on the elbows were both Ralph Lauren.

"Victor and Leslie Ackroyd," he said. He talked on as I looked down my list. "Leslie and I are so excited about this weekend. We both love a mystery and knitting, of course, too. We belong to the Santa Clara Yarn and Wine group, or as we call it, *Stitch and Sip*." I noticed that he was leaning on a walking stick and he rushed to explain. "I have a bum leg from an accident. But don't worry, I'll be able to keep up with the activities." His eye went to the back of the room and settled on the group in red shirts around the pool table. Even from the distance *Glucon* in white letters was visible. Victor made a disgruntled noise and mumbled something about they even had con in their name. As they moved on, I heard Leslie complaining to him that he'd spoken for both of them.

"You always do that and I hate it," she said in a sharp tone. He rocked his head as if he'd heard it all before and gave her an apology in a monotone.

"We're next," a woman said in an excited tone. "Sandra and Bruce Elliott. We're a hybrid couple. I'm the knitter, but we both love mysteries." She leaned closer. "You have no idea how hard it was to get him here. We have our own printing business," she said. "It's only because we had to shut down while they do some repairs that I got him to leave. When he's not working, he just watches TV. I finally convinced him that it would be nice to actually be part of the action instead of just watching it." She leaned even closer. "Let me apologize in advance for him. He's a bit of a complainer."

Bruce apparently had decided no hair was better than just a little and had shaved his head, though a shadow of his hair line was still apparent. He was looking around the large room. "Where's the TV?" Then he seemed to answer himself. "I suppose they're just in the rooms. What about streaming and premium channels?" *How about no channels.* I cringed and tried to think of what to say. Vista Del Mar was unplugged. There was no cell reception, WiFi or TV. I always tried to make that clear to everyone who signed up for a retreat, but somehow not everyone got it. I broke the news to Bruce and his face squeezed into upset. "What, no TV anywhere? What kind of place is this?" He looked around and then at his wife. "What did you sign us up for?"

"Bruce, I told you you'd be too busy to watch TV," she said.

"That's not the same as telling me there is no TV," he grumbled.

"It'll do you good to actually do something instead of just watching other people do things." Her voice had gone from attempting to smooth things over to sounding annoyed.

"I hope the food is at least good," he said, looking at me with a dare.

Sandra tried to pull him with her as she moved on to the manager. He turned back to me. "You do know to count me out from the knitting. Yarn is strictly her thing. I thought I could watch TV while she did her knitting."

I assured him that he wouldn't be required to knit and that there were other activities at Vista Del Mar he could do. I thought his eyes would roll out of his head when I mentioned birdwatching.

Kevin St. John gave them a quick greeting. I'm sure he didn't want to deal with Bruce's wrath. It didn't matter because Bruce had zeroed in on Lucinda, seeing she was in a waitress outfit, and was demanding to know what the menus were. He was ranting on about not wanting any of that vegan stuff or portions that looked like they were for a Barbie doll, when a single woman stopped next to me. I'd learned from Mary Smith's reaction and this time I didn't ask if she was alone.

"Rose Wilburn," she said, looking at my list of names. She had sharp features and brown hair that swung forward and hid her face as she pointed out her name on the list. She seemed like late thirties or early forties. She was either reserved or tense and I imagined by the end of the weekend I'd know if she was one or the other or maybe both. She let out an exasperated sigh and pulled out a plastic clip, using it to pull her hair back before she started asking questions.

"How is it going to work? Will I just stumble over the body? Is it going to be a real person or a dummy? There's no problem taking pictures, is there?" I'd barely nodded when she held up her phone and took a picture of Madeleine's shoes. Then she went back to asking questions.

I waited until she took a breath before trying to answer and said what I'd told the others about getting more information when we met up in the café. Just before she moved on, she looked down at the list. "You do have it that I'm a vegan." I nodded and she moved on reluctantly and seemed unhappy that I hadn't answered all her questions.

Another lone woman came up to me. "Manda Oliver," she said, tapping the list. I already knew she wasn't one of my people by the red shirt. I had to explain again that it was a special event only open to attendees. She didn't take it well and I was doing my best to keep calm and explain it again, when I sensed someone behind me, reading over my shoulder. I turned just enough to see who it was out of the corner of my eye. It was the plain-looking guy from the night before who'd been hitting on the woman in the sweats.

"What's all this about?" he said, checking out the line of greeters and the few people waiting. I started to explain the special event, but his attention suddenly went elsewhere. When I followed his gaze, I saw that the woman from the night before was walking toward the door to the gift shop at the back of the room. She was wearing a set of beige sweats this time, but the black ball cap was the same. I wondered if I should suggest that he give up on her after the way she'd responded. But it was none of my business and maybe he was one of those guys who was turned on by women who didn't want him.

I hoped he wouldn't try hitting on the women in my group. But that wasn't my business either as long as he didn't make it a problem if someone wasn't interested. I watched as he neared the gift shop and then made a last-minute detour and joined the red-shirted group playing pool.

I was still watching him as two women approached. They seemed to be arguing about something to do with their room. And then it went into one of them criticizing the other one about spending too much time on her hair. When I got a look at them, I could tell by the similar build and the way they moved that they were related, but their arguing narrowed it down to a mother and daughter. I knew about that.

"Is there a problem with your room?" I asked, which seemed odd since they hadn't even seen it yet.

"Just that I didn't realize my daughter had us in one room. I really need my own room. I have trouble sleeping and like the windows closed and she likes them open," she said. She gave their names as Jenn and Emily Van Ness.

The daughter was rolling her eyes. She touched her mother's long hair and shook her head. "If you'd get it cut like mine, it would just be shower and shake instead of the whole production you do. Or you could just not fuss about it for the weekend."

Jenn patted the cascade of perfect ripples of dark brown hair touched with a hint of cherry. "To each their own. I don't tell you how to wear your hair or that you really ought to start using moisturizer now when you're young." They continued to argue and I waited for a break to check them on the list. They seemed to have an issue about everything. The trip was a gift from the daughter and the mother was upset that she hadn't known where they were going until they'd gotten on the plane.

"I knew you lived in the area before I was born and I thought it would be nice. Now that you're a widow, you need to get out and do things. I know it's hard being on your own. That's why I thought it would be fun to do this together."

"I'm sorry for your loss," I said.

"Thank you, it's been over a year now. When it stops being the first Christmas and first birthday alone, it gets a little easier. But I'm still faced with what I'm going to do with my life. Not so easy when you're in your fifties."

I noticed their suitcases. Emily's was a carry-on and Jenn's, judging by its size, must have been checked. The daughter saw me looking at it. "I tried to get her to take something smaller."

Jenn did a flourish with her hand. "It takes a lot of equipment to keep this up." I tended to side more with the daughter. Pretty as her hair was with the perfect ripples, I could only imagine how long it would take to get that look with some kind of tool.

"I just want you to love this weekend," Emily said. "We both like knitting and mysteries."

"We want you both to love this weekend," I said. "How about I give you each your own room?"

"Thank you, my dear. Now I can primp in peace," the mother said, giving my arm a squeeze. Madeleine stepped in to introduce herself and they were both delighted with her old-time appearance.

. "It looks like I'm the end of the line," a lone man said. He had silver hair and a neatly trimmed beard and seemed to be taking everything in as he inched his way toward me. "I'll tell you the truth," he said, putting his hand over the sheet on my clipboard. "I marked my profession as a librarian. I am a librarian, that's not a lie, but I left out my other profession, the one that drew me to sign up for this as soon as I heard about it. I'm Talulah Barnsdale," he said in almost a whisper. It took him a moment to realize the name meant nothing to me. He deflated a little. "You really don't know who Talulah Barnsdale is. The mystery writer with the series about Nellie Robinson, the park ranger with a cat who reads minds. I wanted to be part of the mystery for once instead of creating it. And having knitting mixed in, well, Nellie is an avid knitter and I have to admit that I have sort of been faking that part. All I ever say is that she took out the ball of yarn and her needles and began to knit. I thought it would be great if I actually knew how to handle a pair of them." He looked ahead to the greeting committee, recognizing where the idea had come from. "I love this. Maybe I'll borrow it and put it in one of my books. This is going to be fun," he said, giving me a last look just as Madeleine came by to introduce herself. He reacted with a delighted smile before moving down the line. Since he was the last, it was easy to figure out that he was Milton Carruthers.

I did a last check of the list and let out a sigh of relief as I realized everyone was accounted for.

Now that they had all gone into the café, the reception line fell apart. Kevin St. John went back to his station behind the counter. Lucinda left for the restaurant, promising to be back to set up the afternoon tea. Cloris stayed loose because she was going to help me get the group checked in to Vista Del Mar. Cory and the housekeeper went off to attend to their duties.

Madeleine seemed at loose ends, and instead of going into the café with the others was hanging around me.

I was so wrapped up in greeting everyone in that I hadn't noticed that a key someone wasn't there. How about our victim. I'd barely completed the thought when Sammy came in.

"I'm sorry I'm late," he said. He started to go into detail, but when I heard the word *bladder*, I knew whatever he'd been doing had to do with the medical practice he was working in and I stopped him and said it was okay.

He was dressed in a tuxedo with the tie loose. I had already decided not to have him in the line of greeters. There were other plans for him.

Chapter 8

My group had moved on to the café and I stopped in the doorway to observe for a moment, trying to get a handle on who was who. I was glad I'd given them name tags to fill out because I'd already forgotten their names, except that I did remember the man with the silver beard was Talulah Barnsdale. I'd already decided to use an old trick I'd come up with. I found that it was easier to keep track of my people by using both their first and last names. I was also waiting for Madeleine and Cloris to catch up with me.

"When is it supposed to start?" Mary Smith said, introducing herself to the Elliotts, or as they called themselves, the hybrid couple. Sandra Elliott shrugged and said she didn't have a clue.

Bruce looked at the white-haired woman, tilting his head as if to get some insight into her. "Mary Smith. Really, you'd think they'd come up with a better name," he said and asked her if she was the killer.

"It's my real name and I'm not the killer, but if I was, I certainly wouldn't tell you."

"You think the killer is one of us?" Milton Carruthers said, looking around at the nine people spread around the tables that had been pushed together.

Victor Ackroyd leaned his walking stick against the table and addressed everyone in earshot. "C'mon, we know it's going to be the butler. It's always the butler. We own a design business and I'm an expert in seeing patterns."

"Butler? There wasn't a butler in that reception line unless it was the guy with the round face in the black suit, or they went for a female butler and it was the woman in the blue jacket," Emily Van Ness said.

Rose Wilburn was fiddling with something on the table and taking a picture of it as she listened to them go on. "You people are ridiculous, accusing each other of being the killer and someone else saying it was done by the butler when we haven't even begun. I for one want to get my money's worth and go through the whole shebang and follow the clues instead of trying to figure out how the person who arranged it thinks."

I took that moment to make my entrance. Madeleine and Cloris came in behind me. Cloris caught up with me, but Madeleine didn't seem to know where she belonged—at one of the tables with the retreaters or with Cloris and me. Finally, she went to lounge against the counter.

As soon as the group saw me, they were like butter on toast, asking questions. I was just telling them that we were going to hand out everything and Cloris would get them checked in, when there was a loud bang and everyone looked toward the sound.

Sammy was standing in the doorway and smacked his fist against the frame, making a repeat of the noise. He lurched into the room, banging into a chair as he did and then stopped and looked around as though he was looking for someone. His eye stopped on Cloris.

"Hey, babe, where's that room you promised me? I just flew in from Monte Carlo and I need some shut-eye before the card game." Because of all the magic shows, Sammy was good in front of a crowd and he was hamming it up.

Cloris blinked a few times as she got into character and let out an indignant sigh. "You're drunk. El Bosso better not see you." She shook her head in a disgusted manner. "I know about you and the house-keeper Jane."

Sammy hiked himself up and made a coin appear out of her ear. "I'm a master at magic. I can do it drunk or sober," he said. "Jane means nothing to me. It's over anyway. You should know I'm a love 'em and leave 'em kind of guy. I always come back to you." She went to slap him, but he grabbed her wrist and pulled her to him and kissed her.

That wasn't in the script, but apparently Sammy had taken it seriously when I said he was free to ad-lib. It got a little hot and there seemed to be an actual spark between them. I didn't believe either of them was that good an actor. Abruptly she pulled away and gave him a surprised look. "You've used that line on me too much," she said. "I know the truth. We're done."

Sammy stood up straight and his gaze settled on her. "Oh, no, we're not. You'll never be free of me."

She put her hand on her hip as if struggling to find the right pose. "We'll see about that."

Sammy stormed out, pulling out a bunch of silks from his pocket and leaving a trail behind him. The combination of surprise and melodrama had the group transfixed No one moved and they didn't seem to quite know what to do. "And . . . scene," Cloris said, gazing out at them.

Sandra Elliott began to clap her hands in applause. The rest of them joined her. Cloris wasn't sure what to do and ended up taking a bow.

As soon as the clapping stopped, the conversations started up and I realized the charade had been a success and brought them together. I heard people start bragging to each other about what podcasts they listened to and what murder party game they'd solved. Milton Carruthers stayed in the background and I wondered if I should try to help him join in. The silver-haired man had seemed friendly and likeable when I'd greeted him in, but now I wondered if he was one of those people who was shy in a group. Since he was a mystery writer, I was sure the group would probably welcome his insight. I decided to let him be for the moment.

Sandra Elliott had taken out a ball of light green yarn and what looked like the beginning of a baby blanket. She began knitting with expertise, which meant she could keep her needles going without having to watch every stitch. Jenn Van Ness had stopped next to her and watched how her needles rushed through a row.

"I used to be able to knit like that. I should probably brush up on my skills now that I'm a widow. I hate the way that sounds. As if I should grab my needles and wrap myself in a shawl and sit in a rocker."

"I couldn't help but overhear," Mary Smith said. "You're too young for that. Being in your fifties isn't old anymore." Then she stopped, seeming uncomfortable. "I hope I didn't offend you by mentioning what I think is your age."

"No offense taken. I know how old I am," Jenn said. "And what it means. Romance and adventure are all in the rearview mirror." I was going to say something about how vibrant she looked in her slim capri pants and tucked in maize-colored shirt. But Mary seemed to be on the case and I let her do the reassuring.

"Look at Julia Roberts. She's in her fifties and still playing romantic leads," Mary Smith continued.

"I suppose you're right," Jenn said and then she had an afterthought. "But if she keeps it up, that scene that's in every romantic comedy where someone has to run somewhere will have to be done on a moving sidewalk." She chuckled at the image.

Emily seemed relieved by her mother's comment. She looked at the rest of the group. "I planned this trip for my mother. She didn't even know where we were going until we got on the plane."

"That seems very thoughtful," Sandra Elliott said. "I hope my daughter does something like that for me someday."

"Over my dead body," Bruce said. There was sudden silence and then he gave the group an exasperated look. "It was a joke, folks. Emily brought her mother here because she's a widow. Get it?"

There were finally a few forced laughs.

I edged into the conversation and turned the subject on to knitting, reminding all of them that there would be a fun knitting workshop. "Not for me," Bruce Elliott bellowed. "We're the hybrid couple, remember. I'm just here for the murder."

There was a moment of nervous laughter and I changed the mood by starting to hand out the folders and goodie bags. Cloris announced she'd be taking care of the paperwork one at a time and they could look through the materials and have a drink while she did the leg work.

I waited until they had their drinks and had looked through everything that I handed out before I did my opening address to them.

"I guess you've all figured that the game is afoot," I said and they all chuckled. "There are some general things to go over before we take you to your rooms." I began with some basics about the place. I always tried to make sure that everyone understood the place was unplugged before they came. But I always went over it again when they were there, as it seemed there was always someone who'd missed it. Bruce Elliott squirmed uncomfortably as I described the total lack of cell service, WiFi and TV. I made sure to point out there were vintage phone booths with pay phones in the Lodge and that there was a message board near the gift shop.

"It's like an electronic detox for the weekend," Rose Wilburn interjected. "There's bound to be some withdrawal from not having access to social media."

"Hopefully you'll be busy enough with the mystery and our knitting workshops that you won't notice," I said, trying to sound positive. Madeleine seemed to have tired of the sidelines and moved from the counter to standing next to me. I wasn't sure how to introduce her and finally just called her Mrs. Maple.

"Remember, I'm the house detective just in case," she said with a lively smile.

"Wait a second," the mystery writer with the silver beard said. "I thought we all get to play detective." The others all chimed in with something similar.

Their fussing was interrupted as Sammy swept into the room again. He seemed sober this time, and on a mission as he marched to the counter, leaned over it, and grabbed Bob by his apron. The barista seemed a little startled and then seemed to remember that this was all an act, and his mild face turned menacing.

"Get out," he yelled at Sammy. "Consider our partnership ended. No one cheats El Bosso and gets away with it."

"You'll regret it," Sammy said in a forced angry tone. "Just remember that I know what I know." The tall hulky man made a theatrical exit.

There was a hush for another moment and Madeleine looked over the group. "I think there's going to be trouble."

Chapter 9

With everyone checked in, the next step was to get them to their rooms. Cloris and I led the way back through the main room, assuring them that their suitcases would be delivered to the building.

Most of them had taken the news about Vista Del Mar being unplugged rather well. Except Bruce Elliott, of course. He was still fussing at his wife for not explaining it to him. I thought that some of his upset was coming from what they'd come here to get away from. All I'd been able to gather was that something happened to damage their printing business and they'd had to shut it down while it went through some costly repairs. Sandra had tried to smooth things over by saying something to the effect that it was what savings were for.

The Sand and Sea building sat on top of a small hill just above the main driveway. It was one of the original buildings from when it had been a camp and had been housing for the counselors. As we stood at the foot of the slope, I caught them eyeing the weathered brown single building with wariness. The wisp of fog being carried in by the ocean breeze added to the brooding atmosphere. I felt a renewed sense of tension. I tried to be clear about the accommodations, but it wasn't the same as seeing that the actual rooms were sparse, to say the least. This time I had the added concern of how Madeleine was going to feel. It was her choice, but just like she was calling her "work" at being Mrs. Maple a job, she wasn't always exactly realistic. I wondered if she'd even seen the guest rooms.

Despite being owners of the hotel and conference center, Madeleine and Cora kept a distance when it came to running it. They did leave most of it to Kevin St. John, except when they wanted to give me a special deal on the rooms or push for Cloris to be made assistant manager. And then it had been mostly Cora. She was the younger sister but seemed to be the one in charge.

I heard bits of conversations going on behind me as Cloris and I led the way up the slope to the building with their guest rooms.

Victor Ackroyd was pointing out the Arts and Crafts details of the assorted structures like the use of local stone. Emily Van Ness was trying to get reassurance from her mother that she was enjoying the retreat so far. I felt for the way she was trying so hard, going on about what fun the scenes with Sammy had been. I had wanted to do the same thing with Madeleine, but she was turning out to be easier to please than I'd thought—but the weekend was still young. I looked back to check on her and she was walking with the group and talking to someone.

There were a few breathless sighs as we reached the top of the slope. Cloris went first to hold the door for them as they came up the few stairs and across the small porch. It was a bit of a struggle for Victor Ackroyd with his walking stick, but it didn't keep him from pointing out that the column holding up the overhang over the porch was made of local stones.

They all stopped in the lobby, which had the inviting look of a living room with a glowing fire and an arrangement of comfortable chairs. It had been personalized with a statue of the Maltese Falcon on the mantel piece and some pictures on the wall. There were plants on a couple of the small tables next to the chairs and a glass bowl of seashells on a table against the wall. "This is the perfect spot when you want to read a book, work on your knitting or enjoy a glass of wine at the end of the day," Cloris said.

"Too bad there isn't a TV," Bruce Elliott said under his breath. His wife shushed him and agreed it would be a nice place to hang out with the other knitters.

Someone noticed the stairway and asked what was upstairs. "More guest rooms," Cloris said. "I'm sorry we couldn't give you the whole building, but we already had reservations. I'm sure they won't bother you. And we have a parlor set aside in the Gulls building that is just for you all."

The plan was that I would take Madeleine to her room and Cloris would take the others to theirs. We all went into the hallway together.

Because the walls were covered in walnut-colored wood, it was dark with maybe a touch of spooky.

I waited until Cloris and her group started down the hall and I turned and went the other way with Madeleine. No matter how much she had said she wanted to be like the others and stay at Vista Del Mar instead of going home to her fabulous Victorian house, I had a hard time believing her. So I stacked the deck.

The building had originally been housing for the camp counselors and the rooms were small and very plain. I found that one of the rooms was larger and guessed it had been for the head counselor. It was on a corner and had more windows and a better view.

Then I'd worked on the interior. With Cloris's help, we took out one of the narrow beds and put in a writing desk. We added a memory foam topper to the cot-sized mattress and switched out the sheets for something less rough. I'd raided the stash of things my aunt had knitted and crocheted and spread a lovely black afghan with pink flowers over the foot of the bed. We'd hung prints and photographs on the usually bare walls, added a small shelving unit with a plant and some old hardcover books along with a jar with some dried lavender flowers and eucalyptus leaves. There wasn't much we could do to the old analog clock radio.

She'd gotten a goodie bag like the rest of them, but I'd left a second round of everything in the room and tucked the lavender sachet in her sheets to give them the relaxing scent.

Even with all of that I gritted my teeth, worried about her reaction as I opened the door and showed her in.

She moved around looking at everything and I couldn't tell by her expression what her reaction was. "I haven't been in one of these rooms in ages," she said finally. "It seems nicer than I remember."

"Except this," she said, standing in the doorway to the bathroom. There wasn't anything I could do to change the tiny room. The shower, sink and toilet barely left space for someone to turn around. She took a step in and pulled back the shower curtain and looked inside. "I usually take a bath, but it will be a new experience for a few days.

"I like it," she said with a smile. All these years and I have never spent a night here before."

Just then there was a blood-curdling scream from down the hall. We both ran out and followed the sound. Everyone else had heard it too and we joined a mad rush toward the room at the end. There wasn't space for everyone to get in the room so they crowded around the open door and peered inside to see who had screamed and why.

Jenn Van Ness was holding her heart and didn't seem to know whether to laugh or be upset that she'd found Sammy and the housekeeper hiding in her closet. "I opened the door and they popped out," she said. He had lipstick marks on his face and rushed away while the housekeeper slung away embarrassed.

Madeleine clapped her hands together with a bright smile. "This is so exciting."

I noticed that Cloris was missing, probably because it would have been awkward when she didn't take part in the scene. I would have liked to have high-fived her for helping me put this together. Madeleine seemed happy, as did the rest of them.

"If you come back to the lobby," I said, "your bags should be waiting." The whole group trooped back to the pleasant front room. The light glinted off the silver buttons on Cory's vest as he guided a cart in from the back entrance. All the suitcases were piled on it.

Before anyone could make a move, Kevin St. John came down the stairs and went to the cart of luggage and pulled out a small black suitcase. He opened and inside there were stacks of bill-sized pieces of paper. The manager feigned shock. "There was supposed to be a million dollars in there. He double-crossed me. He's got the flash drive. Where is he? I'm going to make that magician disappear."

"I just moved the bags, sir," Cory said, putting up his hands in innocence.

"You helped him, didn't you?" the manager said in a menacing voice. Cory hid a giggle as he looked at all of us. Just then the housekeeper reappeared and looked from Cory to Kevin St. John. She whispered "El Bosso" and she and Cory rushed out.

I couldn't speak for Kevin St. John's acting ability, but the group was enchanted. There was laughter and chatter about what had just happened. The manager had a forced smile and did quick bow of his head aimed at Madeleine, and then as he went to leave he showed his real feelings as he shot me a hard look.

Now that they were back to reality, they went to retrieve their bags. I looked up as I heard someone coming down the stairs. At first, I thought it was just another random guest, but then I realized it was the man from the previous night. The same one who'd been hanging around when I was checking people in. He was really bland-looking in the cargo pants and fleece jacket. He had a baseball cap on now, but I remembered his hair as being a light brown with a nondescript cut. It seemed to me if he was hoping to score with the ladies, he ought to up his game.

He looked over our group as he reached the first floor. It must have seemed rather chaotic with all the noise and people pulling out their bags and I thought I should say something.

But when he got to the bottom of the stairs, he mixed in with the crowd. I saw him stop to talk to the woman with the white hair. Mary Smith, the one I'd said was a woman of mystery because she didn't want to give her occupation. I edged closer, curious what they were talking about. All I heard was that he said his name was Gary Moser.

Most of them had their suitcases and were looking to me to say something.

"And now you can all get settled and relax for a bit," I said. "If you look at the schedule, you'll see we have an opening reception that is going to be like an afternoon tea in the parlor in the next building. Then there's dinner in the dining hall followed by a beach walk. After that, who knows?" I said, trying to sound mysterious.

I heard a number of people say they couldn't wait.

Chapter 10

It wasn't even the end of the first day and I was worn out. This was so different from the yarn-only retreats I'd put on before. They'd been a lot more peaceful and there hadn't been the pressure to please Madeleine and support her in her position as Mrs. Maple. I accepted that I would be on the edge of anxiety all weekend.

My people had a break now, but I didn't. I just changed locations. The first stop was the Lodge to check in with my "players." Kevin St. John was already back behind the counter. I forced myself to go up and thank him. He saw that I was alone and dropped the pretense of being friendly. "I hope that was the end of it," he said.

"Actually, it's just the beginning," I said, and I reminded him that my detectives would want to question all the suspects. He pulled out a folder and looked at the paper inside.

"Is this what I'm supposed to say?" he asked. I glanced over it and it had the important information he was to offer.

"You can make up the rest," I said. He shook his head, unhappy with the whole program, but he also knew as long as Madeleine was there, he had to comply.

It was a lot more pleasant to join Cloris, Sammy and Cory, who were sitting around one of the tables near the windows that gave them some separation from the guests.

"Great job, everybody, and I want to thank you again," I said as I joined them.

Sammy was sprawled on the chair and had a canned energy drink in his hand. "I'm trying to rest up for act three. Playing a guy everybody wants to kill is exhausting."

"I loved seeing the look on their faces when they realized I was part of the show," Cory said. The teen seemed energized by it all.

"I think we're a success so far," Cloris said. "I hope there won't be any snags."

Her comment made me think of the guests on the second floor and particularly Gary Moser. I told her about the reaction the woman in sweats had had at his attention.

"Everybody knows the lobby area is shared space and I'm sure they won't mind the changes we made for your group. As for the man—just ignore him. From what you said he walked away as soon as she blew him off."

"I hope you're right," I said as I got up to leave. "Until later." I gave them both a wave.

It felt good to walk outside and not to have to deal with anybody for the moment. The sky had a tinge of apricot, hinting that the sun was up there somewhere and the cool temperature refreshed me as I headed for home.

Julius was watching me from his perch by the kitchen window as I walked up my driveway.

He started his routine as soon as I walked in the door.

"I need a minute," I said to the cat. He gave me a meow, which I took as impatience. We both had our agendas. His was a snack of stink fish and mine was baking some fresh butter cookies for the reception. I put the oven on to preheat and was going to get a glass of water before tackling the stink fish, when there was a light rap at my kitchen door before it opened and Dane stuck his head in.

He was out of uniform wearing a gray T-shirt and a pair of faded-from-wear jeans that hugged his well-toned body. "I thought I'd check to see how it's going."

"It's going, that's for sure," I said with a weary smile.

"Interesting outfit," he said, looking at the white shirt and trousers. "You look like something out of an old movie." I realized I hadn't shown him the outfit before.

"That was the objective," I said. I reminded him of Madeleine's desire to make the weekend seem like something out of a traditional English mystery. "You should see what she's wearing. I'm glad all those suits were in style before my time." The cat jumped down from the counter. "The food we're serving is more interesting, though I had to do research to get it all straight."

I explained that "tea" really meant a small meal. And there were all these variations.

He nodded to show he was listening, but he seemed to have something else on his mind. "How's it going with your actors? You know I could have played the part of a dashing bad boy," he said. "I'm an experienced bad boy, and as for dashing . . ." He struck a pose and we both laughed. "It would be more convincing if I was wearing a tuxedo with the tie hanging loose."

He was teasing, but he sounded almost like he felt left out. It was actually funny to have Sammy playing a bad boy since he was anything but. Dane did have real-life experience. When he'd been taking care of his mother and sister, he acted like a bad boy to the outside world, complete with a motorcycle, slicked hair and negative behavior.

"And if you had, Lieutenant Borgnine would have had you working holidays for the next five years," I said. Julius wasn't having any of our conversation and meowed, giving his tail an annoyed flick as he walked to the refrigerator and I started to follow.

Dane looked at the cat and laughed. "You're such a spoiled kitty," he said. He put up his hand to stop me. "I'll do the honors." Julius watched Dane go in the refrigerator, but the cat didn't seem sure of what was going on until Dane took out the heavily wrapped can, and then Julius did a few figure eights around Dane's ankles.

"So that's what it takes to make you my friend," he said, shaking his head at the cat's fickleness. Dane had tried to make up to the cat a number of times, but Julius seemed to view him as an invader on his turf. But it seemed like things might have changed. "If I knew that was all it was going to take, I would have done this a lot sooner." He made a face at the stench as he said, "Or maybe not." He put a dab of the cat food in the bowl as he talked to the cat. "I hope you realize how lucky you are to have someone care so much about you that she deals with this." He glanced back at me with a question in his eye and I laughed.

"Okay, yes, if you would only eat something with a horrid smell, I'd gladly serve it to you."

"Whew," Dane said, wiping his forehead in mock relief. "I'm glad to know that I'm right up there neck and neck with your cat," he said in a teasing voice. I opened my mouth to explain, but he did it for me in his usual light manner with a touch of melodrama. "I know I can never compete with the sob story Julius has. I'm just a small-town cop who fell for your big-city ways. Whereas the cat was abandoned and Kevin St. John tried to run him down with a golf cart." He let out a sigh and looked at the black cat gobbling his snack. "I guess he'd get my sympathy vote, too." Julius finished and walked away from the bowl. Dane leaned down to give him a stroke along his back. Julius surprised me by letting out a loud purr before turning around and coming back for more pets.

"I think we've really become buds," Dane said, sounding pleased. "I've always been more of a dog person, but that doesn't mean I can't like the right cat.'" He gave Julius a final stroke and went to redo all the wrappings and put the stink fish in a special compartment in case any hint of the stink escaped.

I turned on the oven and waited until the cat food was put away before taking out rolls of cookie dough. "I'm supplying the sweets for the tea. I just have to make some cookies. I already made everything for a trifle and a vegan version of it. I'll assemble them just before they're served. I made sour cream biscuits, too." I pointed out the box on the table. He flipped it open and I offered him one.

"When it comes to baking, you're the best," he said.

"I know, and it's everything else that I'm a flop at." *Flop* was really the wrong word. It was more no interest. I was content with instant stuff and frozen meals. I loved baking, but making a regular meal left me cold. I always kept rolls of the butter cookie dough ready in the refrigerator to slice and bake.

Dane washed his hands and came back to the counter, where I laid out cookie sheets. "What's the plan? Are we going nude or decorated?"

"Actually, I was thinking I'd turn them into sandwich cookies with some buttercream icing in the middle."

"I can be your sous chef," he said. "And you can tell me all about your retreat group. Are there any sinister characters in this group or bossy flossies already trying to take over?" He handed me an apron. "You don't want to mess up your outfit."

"The closest to a sinister character is a guy who isn't even part of my group." I described what Gary Moser had done the night before with the woman in the sweats and he grimaced.

"Maybe he's a weirdo. I mean, Vista Del Mar doesn't seem like the kind of place to go looking for a girlfriend." He shrugged. "Unless you're a bird-watcher or something."

I told him what Cloris had said.

"That sounds right. As long as he keeps his hands to himself, there's no law about him talking to someone. But let me know if you see him get too pushy with anyone—like you."

"I'm going to take Cloris's advice and ignore him. I have enough on my plate just figuring out all the small meals."

"You really want to tell me about them, don't you," he said.

"I spent a lot time getting them all straight. It would be nice to share."

"Go for it, then." He joined me as we both began to slice up the dough.

"The first thing to know is that even though some of them have tea in the name, they're all meals or snacks. I'll go through them chronologically. The elevens are eaten about that time and are like a coffee break with a light snack of a muffin, scone or biscuit. It's kind of like what people in town do when they get one of my muffins. They call it a cream tea if there's clotted cream and jam served with the biscuits or scones." I placed a row of slices on the cookie sheet. "Depending on where you are, the accepted order of which comes first, the jam or clotted cream, changes."

"I didn't know this was such serious business," he said, holding back a smile.

I was determined to finish and moved on to later in the day. "Afternoon tea is supposed to include small finger sandwiches, scones, and some sweet treats served in a casual setting. The difference with high tea is that it's served at the table and is a more substantial meal. And finally there's supper, which is like what we'd call a midnight snack. Something to eat at bedtime."

"That's a lot to keep straight. I hope Madeleine isn't checking for accuracy," he said and we both laughed. We each carried a cookie sheet to the oven.

"Look at us, so comfortable hanging out and working together in the kitchen." He turned to me with an expectant look and I knew what he was doing.

"I get it. Another pitch for us living together." I rocked my head in my hand. "My brain is on overload just keeping those meals straight. And there's the anxiety about pulling off this weekend."

He softened and took me in his arms. "It will be okay. You will serve the clotted cream and jam in the right order and your people will give you a standing ovation on Sunday." He gave me a squeeze. "And then we can talk about living together on Monday."

Dane was persistent if nothing else. He had never given up taking care of his mother when she started drinking again or stopped believing that one day she would stay sober permanently. He was still his sister's keeper, too. He'd been looking after her since they were kids, and he knew she was likely to show up when her life fell apart. And he was not going to give up on us being together, no matter what excuse I came up with. But I didn't think he realized that he'd met his match. I was just as insistent about keeping my options open.

We made pink icing and spread it between the cookies. Then he helped me pack them between layers of waxed paper in a square tin.

"I'm off to put on the spaghetti sauce and give a karate lesson," he said. "Let me know if you want me to bring you a plate." Dane really was the ultimate good guy. He had turned his garage into a mirror-walled studio and offered free karate lessons and more to local teens. The *more* was a place to hang out and get advice, along with plates of spaghetti oozing with his homemade sauce. I always said it was so good you wanted to lick the plate. He had rescued me from the land of frozen food by supplying me with mounds of pasta. My stomach gurgled just thinking about it.

We parted with a hug, which we both ended quickly since we had places to go.

Chapter 11

The sun had made a surprise appearance and my shadow accompanied me as I went up the Vista Del Mar driveway pulling the wheeled bin stocked with the tin of cookies and the box of biscuits. Lucinda was bringing the rest, including the ingredients for the regular trifle and the vegan version, which I would assemble at the last minute. It wasn't really a traditional thing to serve at tea, but the dessert made of layers of cake, jam, fruit, pudding and whipped cream was very English.

I went over the rest of the menu. It had become an issue to consider what people ate or didn't eat. No one had checked that they needed gluten-free food, but there was a vegan in the group. It still amazed me how being a vegan had gone from something obscure to at least one in every crowd. The good point to it being not so rare was that substitutions were easily available, so we could serve cucumber sandwiches with a layer of plant-based cream cheese, which seemed like a contradiction to me, like nonfat cream cheese. The vegan trifle wouldn't be an exact replica, but close enough. I'd made a vegan vanilla cake and had cubed it. There would be layers of the cake, whipped coconut cream and fresh strawberries.

When Lucinda and I were discussing the arrangements, we'd considered whether to go all out and have fancy cups and saucers, but the thought of people juggling a cup and saucer along with a plate of food while attempting to eat and drink seemed a little too much. We simplified it down to the saucer-less white cups the Blue Door used and plates big enough to set the cups on.

The afternoon sun had enticed everyone outside and I was tempted to join them as they headed to the boardwalk. I was so used to the clouds that I'd forgotten how nice it was to see a blue sky and feel the warmth of the sun. Even the brown weathered-looking buildings appeared less moody in the golden light.

Just as I was beginning to have that feeling that everything would be fine, Kevin St. John came outside and focused on me. It was pretty obvious that he checked the space around me to see if Madeleine was nearby and he'd have to be on his best behavior. His moon-shaped face hardened when he saw she wasn't around.

"Ms. Feldstein," he said in an angry tone. "We've got a problem. I found one of your retreaters in the business area. The woman with the white hair. She said she was looking for clues and waved an open manila envelope.

"That's ridiculous. The 'murder' hasn't happened yet," I said in a concerned tone.

"You didn't put clues in the business area, did you?" he demanded, waiting to pounce if I said I had.

"They got a sealed envelope in their folders that said it wasn't to be opened until tomorrow. I thought I was dealing with adults who had some patience," I said. "There are no clues in the business area either." I paused. "I'll make sure they know."

"And Cora Delacorte was here looking for her sister. I didn't know what to tell her except that I thought she would be at this tea reception you're having this afternoon. You're using the parlor in the Gulls building, correct?"

I nodded. It seemed a better place than the rather stark meeting rooms we were using for the yarn workshops and crime scene. "Good because that's what I told her."

I thanked him again for his help and told him how good he'd been in his scene. I thought he didn't care, but his expression brightened. "Do you really think so? I thought I captured the essence of the character."

"Absolutely," I said with a completely straight face.

The Gulls building was next to the Sand and Sea building and had the same weathered brown shingles, but the Gulls building had a bigger common area that was divided into two parlors closed off with French doors. The parlors had a different look than the lobby of the Sand and Sea building. They were done in dark colors and felt like cozy dens with sofas and easy chairs spread over thick carpeting. The fireplaces gave off a warm glow.

Lucinda was already setting up when I got there.

She'd taken a long table against one wall to use for the refreshments. Urns with coffee and tea sat at one end with the white cups we'd decided on. A bottle of sherry with small glasses was set up nearby. Lucinda had gotten several of the three-tiered stands I'd seen on PBS shows. She'd put plates with doilies on all the levels. "This is for sweets," she said, pointing out one of them. I began to put out the cookies and biscuits. She had brought butter and jam for the biscuits. "We didn't say it was a cream tea," she said with a chuckle.

I took the two glass bowls and the containers of ingredients and began to assemble the trifles. She was setting out finger sandwiches and putting the vegan ones on a separate plate as she asked me for an update.

I described Sammy's first grand entrance and the shock on all their faces. Then I mentioned the kiss. "It wasn't scripted," I said. "And there seemed to be some heat there."

"Sorry I missed it." Then her smiled faded. "Are you upset about it?" she asked, and I had to think about it.

"Truth?" I asked and she nodded. "Bittersweet is probably the best way to describe it." I was going to go into more details of my feelings but was glad to drop it when Rose Wilburn came in. She stopped in the middle of the room and looked around, and then she came to inspect the table.

"I expressly said that I would need vegan food," she said in a tense voice.

"No problem." I pointed her to the plate with the vegan finger sandwiches and the bowl with the vegan trifle. "Oh," she said, almost seeming disappointed that she couldn't make a fuss. I encouraged her to help herself. She took out her phone and snapped photos of the two vegan items before putting a dab of the trifle on a plate and taking several of the finger sandwiches. Then she tried a tentative taste of the trifle and her eyes widened in surprise.

"This is actually delicious." She picked up a finger sandwich and opened it to see what was inside.

"It's cashew cream cheese and cucumber," I said. She smiled as she tasted it. She took out her phone and began to take more pictures. First of the table, and then she made up a plate with food. She added a fork and napkin and photographed it from above. I heard her say something about vegan heaven. The main thing was she seemed happy.

The others began to come in. They all did what Rose had done—stopped in the middle of the room and looked around before heading to the table of treats.

I tried to greet everyone and make them feel welcome. Victor Ackroyd spent more time looking around the room than the others. He'd said they had a design business, which probably accounted for his added interest. I couldn't tell if he liked the room or not. Leslie Ackroyd went right to the table and was making up plates for them, saying they'd missed lunch. Jenn Van Ness poured some sherry in one of the saucer-less cups and retreated to a seat by the fireplace, while her daughter got them a plate to share.

Bruce Elliott was talking at his wife about something as they came in. Judging by what I'd seen of him, I guessed it was a complaint. Milton Carruthers came in on his own followed by Mary Smith. I wondered if I should take her aside and mention that envelope she'd opened too soon or that the business area was off-limits, but then I saw something that made me forget about all that. She wasn't alone. Gary Moser had come in with her and was clearly "with" her. He'd taken off the baseball cap and I had a better view of his face. His expression was noncommittal as he surveyed the room. The woman the night before had been younger and more attractive than Mary Smith and maybe he viewed the white-haired woman as a placeholder until he found someone better.

He seemed to be trying to stay in the background. I remembered what Cloris had said about ignoring him and that seemed the best thing to do under the circumstances. If she brought him to the yarn workshop, I would say something.

Madeleine made an entrance having changed into another suit.

This one was pale blue and made me glad that styles had changed. The straight skirt and jacket with a peplum appeared restrictive and certainly wouldn't go with my sneakers.

She glanced around offering a smile to everyone before she helped herself to some food, She was blissfully enjoying the trifle when Cora Delacorte walked in. She actually fit in perfectly with the tan Chanel suit, black pumps and green eye shadow. Her blondish hair had the "just been to the beauty salon" look of rigid poof. She walked directly to her sister and pulled her aside. Only I could hear their exchange.

"When I heard you'd left with a suitcase, I was worried that you'd been kidnapped. It was highly undignified, but I felt obligated to notify the police." She glared at her sister. "You have no idea how distasteful it was to hear from that man in the rumpled jacket that my sister was staying at Vista Del Mar and pretending to be a detective. Have you lost your mind? How could you do all this without telling me? I would have stopped it before it got this far."

Madeleine slipped back into her old self and seemed to grow smaller as her sister bullied her. "The Delacorte sisters don't do common things like stay here. At the very least you could have stayed in the owner's bungalow. You should come with me now. I have a driver with the golf cart waiting. Your place is already set for dinner."

Everybody was watching without being able to hear and I don't think they knew if it was real or part of our mystery game. Madeleine seemed to be dithering and I wondered if I should step in. Cora leaned in and said something only for Madeleine's ear and our Mrs. Maple turned back into the dutiful sister and let Cora lead her out.

They all looked at me when the two women left and I had to say it was a family matter and not part of the mystery. When I checked the group, I saw that Gary Moser had left, and the way Mary Smith looked at the empty seat next to her made me think she'd expected him to stay.

A moment later, Sammy came barreling into the room. He walked straight up to Lucinda.

"I know what you tried to do. No one double-crosses the famous magician Luis Montana. Give me the jewels now." He held out his hand as if she would drop them in.

Lucinda came from behind the service table and stopped next to him. He towered over her, but she didn't seem intimidated. "They are long gone. It's your problem now. Wait until El Bosso finds out you don't have them." She made a motion as if a knife was cutting her throat. "You better make a run for it before he finds you." With that Sammy made a very theatrical exit.

A moment later Kevin St. John came in with Cory following him. My compliment must have meant something to the manager, because he actually put himself into it this time. He looked around the room with a menacing stare. "Where is he?" he demanded, looking at Lucinda.

The woman in the black maid's uniform curtseyed to the two of them. "El Bosso, he's gone. He double-crossed us all. He has the jewels and the money."

They were all hammy, but the group ate it up.

"Uh-oh," Victor said, wiggling his eyebrows in a melodramatic fashion. "I think we know who our victim is going to be." He leaned on his walking stick as he looked around the room for their reaction.

Milton Carruthers seemed content to stay an observer and let the rest of them voice their opinions about what Victor Ackroyd had said. I doubted he had even told the group he was a mystery author, writing under a woman's name. I did notice that he seemed to be jotting down some notes.

I was going to wait for the comments to finish, but when there was no lull in the conversation, I interrupted to make announcements about the upcoming activities. An old-fashioned bell would announce that dinner was available in the Sea Foam dining hall. The group would have a walk to the beach afterward. I didn't say the point was to get them off the grounds while the murder was set up to be discovered on their return. I eased in a reminder that the envelope of clues wasn't to

70

be opened until the victim was found, and I refused to confirm or deny who the victim was going to be. I looked in Mary Smith's direction as I said that certain areas were off-limits and then specified the business area. Her face showed no reaction. What did that mean?

Chapter 12

"Do you think Madeleine is gone for good?" Lucinda asked. The group had cleared out for some free time before dinner, leaving the two of us to clear up after the reception. "She seemed so in charge of herself being Mrs. Maple, I thought she was past letting her sister run things."

"Old habits die hard," I said. I'd personally witnessed Madeleine take one step forward to catch up on all that she'd missed by being so sheltered and then take two steps back. "It's really a shame since she was the one who wanted me to add the murder mystery to the usual yarn retreat."

"Don't you mean commanded," Lucinda said.

"I was trying to be nice. But yes, she did insist on it, and if she's out of it now, it was a waste of a lot of planning."

"And there's something else to consider," my boss and friend said. "You told me that Kevin St. John went along with the whole charade only because of Madeleine since she's an owner of the place. If she's gone, what happens?"

I cleared off the leftovers into a container as I considered what she'd said. "I'm sure he'll be less compliant." I let out a sigh thinking about what it would be like dealing with him for the rest of the weekend without Madeleine as a chip. "It's too late to make any changes. The only thing to do is to keep going forward and hope for the best."

She gave me a supportive hug before she took off.

I took some of the leftovers and had a picnic on one of the benches along the boardwalk. I could have eaten with my group in the dining hall, but I needed the time to regroup, and sitting alone as it was getting dark with the sound of the ocean seemed to be just what I needed. I felt wrung out already and the murder hadn't even happened.

It was completely dark when I went to the Lodge. Cloris gave me a thumbs-up that everything was still a go. And I went to collect my people for the big event.

The lobby of Sand and Sea was empty and I grabbed a seat with a nice view of the fireplace while the group trickled in. When I saw Victor Ackroyd with his walking stick, I suddenly wondered how he'd managed on the sand. He'd said he had a bum leg from an injury.

"No need for concern," he said. "I'll be fine." As if to prove it, he held the stick up and took a dancing step across the floor. His wife, Leslie, gave him a panicked look and ordered him to put the stick down.

"Anyone might think you don't really need it," she said in a terse tone.

Rose Wilburn came in and glanced around the group. She made a move toward Mary Smith then detoured, as if she was worried they would be paired up since they were the two single women. She eyed Milton Carruthers but gave him a dismissive shrug as she stopped next to the Elliotts. I chuckled at how excited Bruce got having a free ear to complain to. Sandra appeared only too glad to have someone else to listen to him go on about how the soup at dinner wasn't hot enough and the meat loaf was tasteless.

There was something very proper about Mary Smith's appearance with the sleek cut of her white hair and the neat look of her pants suit, but this was also the person who'd gone sneaking around the business area and opened the clue folder early. In addition, I had my doubts if that was her real name and wondered if there was a way I could get a look at her driver's license. Then I chided myself for bothering with it. What did it matter who she really was?

Jenn Van Ness seemed deep in thought as she waited in one of the easy chairs. From what she'd said, being a widow and wondering what came next weighed on her mind. It was thoughtful of her daughter, Emily, to have brought her on this weekend in an attempt to divert her troubled thoughts.

"Time to go," I said, moving toward the door and waving my arm for them to follow me. They sensed that the mystery was afoot and there was the sound of excited conversation as they trailed behind me.

The grounds of Vista Del Mar were very dark at night with only some low-to-the-ground lighting along the assorted pathways. I was glad for the scarf I wore because the night air cut right through my sweater. To add to the atmosphere, fingers of fog were drifting in from the water. I heard Milton Carruthers say it was the perfect scene for a murder.

I knew the grounds by heart and led them all to the boardwalk that protected the sandy area on the edge of the Vista Del Mar property. The sand was silky and practically white, broken by dark silhouettes of bushes and plants.

I left them to their conversations and enjoyed feeling the fresh moist air on my face. To make the walk take longer, I led them to the boardwalk loop that ran through the hilly dunes.

The fog had settled in the low spot between the sandy slopes and we were surrounded in the white haze. The loop took us back to the main path and we continued on to the beach. As we hit the sand I looked back, curious if Victor Ackroyd had stopped before the sand, but I saw nine silhouettes, which meant he had stayed with the group.

The waves were barely visible as they rolled up on the shore. I sensed the group was getting impatient and couldn't stall any longer. It was time to go back.

Even though I knew what was coming, I had a sense of nervous tension. I led the way back to the Sand and Sea building, knowing there would be a last-minute detour. As we neared the building, I got ready to say my line, but I saw a figure outside one of the windows looking in. "How could I have forgotten," I said with mock dismay. "I need to show you where the yarn workshop is being held." I moved them back on the path and took a last glance at the figure at the window. There was just enough light to see that it was Gary Moser. Was he a Peeping Tom, too?

"The building is called Cypress," I said as we approached the single-story structure that was nestled in an area between the buildings that housed all the guest rooms. It was so dark that with the lights off, it almost disappeared into the growth around it.

"There are two meeting rooms and we have the nicer one. I'll show you the other one so you'll see that ours is much cozier." I heard a slight quiver in my voice as I kept to the script that we'd come up with. Lucky for me that with all the careers I'd tried, I hadn't been interested in acting. There was no question I would have been a dud. I opened the main door. "Let me show you the room that isn't ours," I said in a false bright tone. The door was open to the larger room but it was pitch dark. I reached for the switch on the wall and the overhead fixture lit up the room.

I heard a yelp of surprise and realized it was coming from me. Even though I had known what to expect, it was still a shock to see Sammy lying on the floor with an oozing red stain on his white shirt. The knife was on the ground next to him in the midst of a pool of red.

The group edged closer. "Really? Ketchup?" Bruce Elliott said with a groan after he touched the red liquid. "It would have seemed more authentic if you'd gotten some real blood, like from a cow." He went on about the color and the smell and I felt my stomach beginning to churn.

Rose Wilburn began to laugh hysterically as she held up her phone. "I instinctively tried to call nine-one-one. Luckily, there's no cell service."

She was right about that. I could just imagine if she'd gotten through and a bunch of uniforms along with Lieutenant Borgnine arrived.

Once I was over the original shock, I suggested that they have a better look. They moved in close and hovered over Sammy. He was doing his best cadaver pose, but I could see his eyes start to flutter as he sensed the crowd.

"Don't worry, you'll have more time to check for clues tomorrow when you begin your investigation. Once the coroner removes the body there will be a chalk outline and everything else will be left at the crime scene."

They were all taking pictures and trying to get a look at the papers and things scattered around Sammy. I could see that Sammy was losing it, and unless it was going to turn into investigating a zombie, I had to get them out of there. It took the promise of a round of wine, but I enticed them to go to the Lodge. Just as we got outside, a golf cart drove up to us, squeaking to a stop as someone hopped off.

"Mrs. Maple has returned," she said as she waved for the driver to leave.

"I missed the discovery of the body," she said with a wail.

Chapter 13

"Tell me everything. How was Sammy as the corpse? How did everyone react?" Lucinda asked when I arrived at the Blue Door to do my dessert prep, muffin making, and put together some treats for the next day's special events for my group. The dining area was empty and they were finishing up for the night. Lucinda had changed out of the black uniform and left the white peaked hat behind. Her favorite designer was Eileen Fisher and she was wearing a pair of black peg leg pants and taupe-colored top she'd had for years. The classic lines never went out of style. She looked at her husband, who was pulling the tables around after insisting they needed a more precise arrangement.

She helped me carry everything back to the kitchen, doing her best to ignore that Tag had taken out a yardstick and was measuring the space between the tables. It felt like an endless day and I was beginning to drag. I'd gotten my group a round of wine and told them about the roast and toast that Vista Del Mar put on. I wasn't sure how roasted marshmallows and hot chocolate would be after the wine, but I thought they would enjoy the campfire.

"Sammy was an outstanding corpse," I said with a laugh. "It's a relief that part is over." I set the recyclable grocery bags with the muffin ingredients aside and pulled the butter out of the cooler.

"I hope it wasn't a problem that I left the grounds since I am one of the suspects," she said with a twinkle. I assured her that it wasn't and then started talking about the group.

"I don't know if it's the location or that Vista Del Mar is cut off electronically, but it seems that there are always some of my retreat people who come with secrets or aren't who they say," I said with a shrug. "It's different having so many men. They're so territorial." I shook my head, thinking of the standoff between some of the people in the red shirts and Bruce Elliott and Victor Ackroyd over the pool table. I described the hostile stares that had gone on. "It's hard to believe they were that worked up over who got to play pool. It almost seemed like there was more to it," I said. And then I got to my real worry. "All it takes is one person to stir things up. Bruce Elliott has found fault with everything. He was even unhappy we didn't use real blood. I'm sure he'll find fault with the clues." I had the stand mixer going, creaming the butter and sugar for pound cake. "This is supposed to be fun, a game. It's not like they're trying to solve a real murder," I said. "And how are they going to deal with the yarn workshop? So far, the only one I've seen knitting is Sandra Elliott."

"At least he seemed happy with the tea food," Lucinda said. "Not that he said anything to that effect, but I saw that he came back for seconds on everything but the vegan versions." She helped me take out the measuring cups but stood away when I grabbed the flour sack, not wanting to get a sprinkling on her clothes.

"It's too bad about Madeleine," she said, "since she's the one behind this whole production."

"She came back," I said with a laugh and explained that she'd snuck out of the house after dinner, telling her sister that she was going to bed early. "She even put pillows under the covers to make it look like she was there. Mrs. Maple is indeed on the case."

Tag stuck his head in the kitchen and seemed agitated, reminding Lucinda that they were off schedule and should be home by now. She gave me an exasperated roll of her eyes and then took a moment to confirm that I'd be making the sour cream biscuits for the next day, and then she let her husband drag her away.

I followed them to the door and locked it before turning on the soft jazz. Dane wouldn't be coming by and was probably still finishing up feeding the karate kids. He had a real way with them and they stayed late talking about their teenage woes. The music and having the place to myself worked their magic and for the first time all day I relaxed.

I was beat when I finally pulled my Mini Cooper into my driveway. The pound cakes were on the pedestal plates under glass domes ready to be served plain or with strawberries and whipped cream. I had left containers with muffins at the coffee spots and brought back one of the containers I used for muffins filled with the sour cream biscuits.

Even at this late hour, Julius was on his perch waiting for me to come in. My mouth began to water when I saw the covered platter of spaghetti sitting by the door. I felt a soft spot for Dane along with ravenous hunger. I was practically sleepwalking as I took care of Julius and then attacked the plate of food.

I awoke twisted in the blanket with Julius sitting on my pillow staring at me with his yellow eyes. I was still in my clothes and by now the white shirt was a mass of wrinkles and the wide-legged pants had rolled up to my knees. I had a feeling I had a tomato sauce mustache from the spaghetti I'd practically inhaled before I crawled into bed. Dane was a sauce genius. I didn't even want to count the number of hours I'd slept. All I knew was that it was too few.

I loved the breakfasts at Vista Del Mar and usually joined my retreat group to feast on pancakes or waffles, egg dishes and fruit. But I was too wrung out from the day before and opted for instant oatmeal after I'd showered and changed. And given Julius his morning dab of stink fish.

Dane had tried to convince me that oatmeal that wasn't instant tasted better and didn't take that long to cook. I'd tried it and agreed he was right, but kept a box of the instant stuff for mornings like this. I did actually brew some coffee. Once I'd gotten used to the real thing, the jar of instant got pushed to the back of the shelf.

The world began to come into focus by the second cup and I was ready to face my group.

There was no sun to brighten the morning, but then no fog either. It was just the business-as-usual flat white sky with no hint of my shadow. I could smell the breakfast I'd missed as I went down the driveway. The spicy aroma of sausage mixed with the scent of pancakes mixed with coffee. It was too late even to get a plate of leftovers. Breakfast was over and the walkway was filled with people crossing the main area as they went on their ways to somewhere else.

The plan was that I would meet my group and walk them to the first yarn workshop. Since they were sure to stop at the crime scene next door, I wanted to be there.

A housekeeper's cart was parked on the path in front of the Sand and Sea building. The lobby was empty, but there was a nice fire going. I sat down to enjoy it while I waited for everyone to appear. The Ackroyds and the Elliotts came in, all looking like they needed another cup of coffee. Milton Carruthers joined us, seeming more alert. I was going to ask about the others when a scream cut through the air. Not just a scream, but a blood-curdling scream that seemed to come from somewhere on the second floor.

Milton Carruthers was standing next to me. "Another surprise," he said with a flash of his eyebrows. "Is it a double murder?" He rushed ahead and went up the staircase with the rest of us following. I squeezed around them to get to the front. Unless Cloris had decided to surprise me by adding to the plans, there was only supposed to be one victim. The walls of the hall were encased in dark brown wood, sucking out all the light, but at the same time making the light coming from an open doorway that much more visible. I tried to up my speed and get there first, which was a challenge because even Victor Ackroyd and his walking stick was rushing to keep up with me.

I looked in the open doorway and the housekeeper was in the middle of the room staring at the open door to the bathroom. I stopped next to her to share her view.

A naked Gary Moser was lying half out of the tiny shower twisted in the pale green plastic curtain. There was no blood and he wasn't moving. I made a move toward him, but Milton held me back and pointed to the ground. An orange extension cord was attached to something black that was touching Gary's arm.

Chapter 14

Kevin St. John pushed his way through and ordered us out. I heard a murmur of "El Bosso" coming from my group as we moved out of the room and back down the stairs.

"This one looks a lot more authentic," Victor Ackroyd said when we returned to the lobby. There was a round of nervous laughter as more of them agreed.

"They even got some 'cops' to come," Bruce Elliott said as several uniforms came through the door. The housekeeper who'd let out the scream was standing by the stairway and pointed them up. Lieutenant Borgnine came in last and looked around at the crowd and his gaze stopped on me.

"Don't tell me," he said in a weary voice. "Is this connected to the mystery weekend? What happened? Somebody here overreacted and thought the body was real?" He shook his head. "I told you Cadbury PD wasn't going to be involved."

As usual he was dressed in a rumpled-looking herringbone tweed sport coat. With his squat build and short neck, he reminded me of a bulldog or a fireplug with a head. His demeanor was as bristling as his short salt-and-pepper hair as he stared at my assembled group.

One of the uniforms came rushing down the stairs. "Lieutenant, you better come up here."

"Now what," he muttered under his breath as he cut through my group and went up the stairs. I heard a siren growing louder and just as the sound became ear-piercing, it cut off. A moment later a man and woman in dark blue uniforms came in with their equipment. Jenn and Emily Van Ness had just walked into the common area and rushed to get out of their way as the EMTs pushed a gurney toward the stairs

"She really went all out," Sandra Elliott said to her husband. "But I suppose you'll find fault with it anyway."

Rose Wilburn had her phone out and was taking pictures. Kevin St. John came down the stairs, waving his hands at us and ordering us to go outside. He focused on me. "Don't you have some activity you're late for?"

In all the commotion, I'd forgotten I'd come to fetch them for the yarn workshop. As soon as I mentioned where we were going, Bruce Elliott reminded everyone that he was only there for the mystery. But after a pause he changed his mind. "But maybe I'll tag along for a few minutes since there's no TV."

Mary Smith was standing on the path holding a paper cup of coffee as we all came out. "What's going on? Is everybody okay?"

"Where's Mrs. Maple?" Leslie Ackroyd asked, checking over the group as they assembled next to the white-haired woman. Just then, the EMTs came out the door of the Sand and Sea building and rolled the empty gurney past us and down the slope to where their ambulance was parked in the driveway.

I considered going back inside to check Madeleine's room, but a uniform was in the doorway streaming yellow tape across it to block entry. I wondered if Cora had discovered the pillows in the bed weren't her sister and returned to force her back home. But Madeleine could have just as easily gone to the café to get a coffee. She wasn't a lost child.

When we reached the Cypress building the door to both meeting rooms was open. For effect a piece of yellow tape was hanging off the doorknob to the crime scene room. Leave it to Cloris to add a touch like that. Sammy's "body" was gone and there was a chalk outline where he'd been sprawled, but everything else was the same. The clues had been spread around the floor. Milton Carruthers started to go inside, but since we were already late for the yarn workshop, I stopped him.

"You can all check it out later," I said, steering everybody to our room. I went in first, realizing that I hadn't done my usual precheck of the room before the first yarn workshop.

Thankfully the precheck was unnecessary and everything was as it was supposed to be. A long table had been set up with chairs around it.

The fireplace was giving off some warmth in the chill morning. I knew I had Cloris to thank for the refreshments on the counter against the wall. She'd brought in air pots of coffee and hot water for tea, along with everything that went with the drinks. She'd even added the tin of butter cookies left from the reception the day before.

"Come in, come in," Crystal said, gesturing to the cluster of people in the doorway.

There was something else that gave me a sense of relief. Even though I kept telling myself that Madeleine, AKA Mrs. Maple, was an adult and I wasn't responsible for her, I smiled when I saw she was sitting at the table next to Crystal's spot at the head. I knew that it wasn't so much a desire to be early for the workshop as it was to spend a few minutes with Crystal. It was slow going, but now that it had been discovered they were family, they were finding they liked each other.

Most of the tension was between Cora and Crystal's mother Gwen. The younger Delacorte sister was used to being in control and she wasn't happy to find out there was a whole slew of relations who could interfere. Her worry was pointless. Gwen Selwyn had no interest in getting in the middle of anything with the Delacorte business. She was busy enough with Cadbury Yarn and helping with her grandchildren. The only reason she had agreed to letting the Delacorte sisters know she was the love child of their late brother was because Cory had inherited his great-grandfather's love of Vista Del Mar. Gwen wanted her grandson to be part of the place.

Crystal wasn't ready to call Madeleine Great-Aunt Madeleine quite yet. And neither she nor Madeleine were ready to have their lives intertwined, but they used events like my retreats to spend time together.

I had to smile at Crystal's getup. She usually looked like a rainbow with layers of brightly colored shirts and socks that deliberately didn't match. The same was true of her earrings. But in keeping with our sometime-in-the-past theme, she'd dressed in a Bohemian style, wearing a vintage gauzy floral-print dress over black leggings and a turtleneck. She had a fragrant gardenia tucked into her curly black hair and as always wore lots of eye makeup. Madeleine had come up with another tweed suit, but the way she looked at what Crystal was wearing, I had the feeling she envied the flowing comfort of her great-niece.

I introduced Crystal Smith to the group as they found chairs around the table and put their things down.

"I heard a siren," Madeleine said. "Did something happen?"

"We think it's a second case for us to solve," the mystery author said, smiling at her. "This one seems a little more authentic." Milton Carruthers nodded at Madeleine's suit. "Mrs. Maple, I must commend you on your outfit. It's just as I imagine what a sleuth would wear."

He looked over the group around the table and explained who he was. "I'm actually Talulah Barnsdale, author of the Nellie Robinson mysteries." He checked their reactions, and when they mostly seemed blank, he continued. "She's a park ranger with a cat who reads minds. If you're interested, I made sure the gift shop has some copies and I'd be glad to personalize them for you."

"Then you probably have an unfair advantage solving the mystery," Bruce Elliott complained. Before I could once again tell him that it wasn't a contest and they'd all be working together, there was the sound of someone clearing their throat in a way that was meant to grab everyone's attention.

Lieutenant Borgnine was standing in the doorway and then he walked in. "I'm going to need a statement from all of you," he said. "Since you are all staying in the Sand and Sea building."

"He's really convincing at playing a Columbo-type cop," Victor said, looking at the detective. "I'd believe he was real if I didn't know he was just another player in the setup."

"I am real," the gruff-looking lieutenant said, opening his jacket to show off his shoulder holster and presenting his badge. They all looked to me and I nodded.

"He is the real thing and the man you saw sprawled on the ground is not part of our scenario."

"You mean that someone is actually . . ." Mary Smith's voice trailed off.

"Deceased is the word you're looking for," the lieutenant said. "And yes, he is and I need to hear from all of you."

"Was it murder?" Leslie Ackroyd said. She was dressed in another Ralph Lauren outfit that would make Lucinda drool. Her husband had snapped to attention as they waited for the cop to speak.

"We prefer to say homicide," the cop said. "And we don't have all the facts yet, which is why we need to speak to each of you."

"Who cares about the dead magician, this sounds more interesting," Bruce Elliott said.

Emily Van Ness put her arm around her mother. "I thought it was just going to be a fun weekend."

Jenn took over the role of comforter and assured her daughter it wasn't her fault the weekend was turning out different than expected.

"I said I need a statement from all of you, not your help." The lieutenant looked at me. "Ms. Feldstein, please keep your people 'investigating' only the fake murder."

"I thought you said you prefer homicide," Rose Wilburn said.

"When it's real, yes," the man in the rumple sport coat said. "But yours is just a game."

It was then that he seemed to notice Madeleine. "Ms. Delacorte," he said with a slight bow of his head to indicate his respect for her.

"For this weekend, I'm Mrs. Maple. Mrs. Julie Ann Maple, lead detective for this group."

The words were barely out and there were protests all around.

"You said we're all in it together," Sandra Elliott said before her husband could jump in.

"Maybe I should explain," I said, hoping to make some peace. "I usually put on retreats that are just about yarn craft. The biggest mystery is what to do about a dropped stitch, but it was Madeleine's—I mean Julie Ann Maple's—idea to add mystery to working with needles and hooks. And to come up with her identity."

"When you start talking about finding killers as being part of a game, that's when I'm out of here," Lieutenant Borgnine said. "We'll be in touch about those statements, and in the meantime please don't talk about it amongst yourselves." He let out a hopeless chuckle as if there was any way he could keep that from happening. As soon as he was gone everybody started talking at once. I looked at Crystal and she shrugged in a hopeless manner.

They were sure a rowdy bunch and I had to get their attention back. I didn't think I could make my voice loud enough to be heard over the din. Dane had a trick he used with the karate kids when they got raucous. Instead of trying to talk over them, he would whisper. Somehow, he managed to get it to work, but I think it required looking at the speaker and seeing their lips move, but not be able to hear them. This crowd was too busy talking to each other to look up at me.

There was one thing left in my arsenal from being a teacher. When I couldn't get their attention using my voice, I dropped a big book on the floor and the sudden loud noise made them freeze. There wasn't a book to drop, but as I looked around the room, I thought of something else. I'd taught about the Bernoulli effect, and I went to open the window. It was already sucking air out of the room when I approached the door and gave it a swing. It slammed shut with a louder bang than any book drop could have made.

Success! There was sudden silence as they all turned toward me as I stood by the closed door. Before I could make use of having their attention, the door pushed open, knocking me out of the way, and Kevin St. John rushed in followed by a cop in uniform and Lieutenant Borgnine. "We heard a gunshot," the manager said, looking at the group around the table and then at me.

"Hands up and whoever's got the weapon better drop it," the lieutenant said.

Everyone complied putting their hands up, looking at the others as if there was actually anybody with a gun.

"Ever hear of the Bernoulli effect?" I said before pointing at the open window and explaining about it creating a sort of vacuum. At least I had everyone's attention and managed to keep it as the three intruders left, giving us all dirty looks as they did.

"Time for knitting," Crystal said with a smile at the absurdity of the abrupt segue from something violent to such a peaceful pursuit. She held up a skein of Dutch-blue yarn and a pair of needles as they reacted with a titter of nervous laughter.

I expected Bruce Elliott to push away from the table with another mention of how he wasn't there for the yarn stuff, but he stayed put. His wife seemed stunned.

It seemed rather anticlimactic after all that had happened, but Crystal went ahead asking if everyone in the group knew how to knit.

"My sleuth, Nellie Robinson, does, but I'm afraid other than reading about things like casting on, knit and purl stitches and such, I'm in the dark." His eye rested on the knitting needles in Crystal's hand. "Well, and I have used metal needles as a murder weapon."

"That won't be part of our lesson," Crystal said as there was another titter of laugher.

Sandra Elliott nudged her husband and he put his hand up. "I'm not really supposed to be in here. We're a hybrid couple. She's here for the knitting, but I came just for the mystery part." He looked around at the others around the table. "But as long as I'm in here, I might as well stay. It's this or watch the people go in and out of the Lodge and pretend they're in a TV show."

"I'm pretty good with a pair of needles," Victor Ackroyd said. "My wife and I are part of the Stitch and Sip group in Santa Clara. It's become quite the thing with the Silicon Valley crowd. Somehow balancing things by doing something with your hands after all that time spent with the digital world."

Leslie added a nod that had an air of superiority about it, as if they'd somehow elevated the ancient yarn craft into something new with previously unknown benefits.

Mary Smith asked for details about the group and who could join.

"It's kind of a closed group," Leslie said in a dismissive tone.

"I think I heard about it on social media," Rose Wilburn said. Then she closed her eyes and seemed upset. "Never mind. It doesn't matter." She blew out her breath and seemed to be trying to calm herself. "I know how to knit and crochet," she said. "But wait, you were just asking who didn't know. Sorry."

"As long as everyone seems to be chiming in," Crystal said, looking at the Jenn and Emily Van Ness.

"I haven't touched it in a while," Jenn said. "But I'm guessing it's like riding a bicycle." She let out a chuckle. "Or at least I'm hoping so."

"If she has trouble, I can help her," Emily said. "This weekend was my idea. I wanted to do something special for my mother because she's going through a lot." Jenn touched her daughter's arm to stop her from going into more detail. I guessed she didn't want to be described as a widow again.

Sandra Elliott didn't wait to be called on. "I knit and belong to a group that meets in a library." She glanced in her husband's direction. "It's my evening out, away from everything and *everyone.*"

I think we all understood who that included. Bruce was unrelenting and it was hard enough to deal with him for this weekend. The thought of living with him made me shudder. But then I wasn't too keen on living with anyone. Maybe if I made Dane understand that, he would realize it wasn't about him. But this was not the time to worry about my living arrangements and I forced my attention back onto the moment.

Crystal patted Madeleine's hand. "Mrs. Maple, I know what level you're at," she said and then turned to address the others. "Now that I know who knits and who needs a lesson, I'll tell you about the project." She held up two blue knitted tubes. "These are hand warmers or fingerless gloves, or as they've become known, texting gloves." She slipped them on her hands and took out her cell phone and demonstrated typing. "Not that you'll be using them this way here," she added as a joke.

She pulled them off and handed them to Madeleine to pass on when she'd looked at them. "They are one size fits most and unisex, along with being easy to make and hopefully quick enough that you may be able to finish them while you're here."

She had another sample to show off. This time, it was a knitted rectangle and she showed how it could be folded and sewed together with a space left open for the thumb. "You can go for a solid color, or if you're more adventurous, you can choose one of the cakes of yarn swirled with different colors." She held up the pair she'd shown me when we first discussed the project. Without waiting for someone to shout out that they didn't match, she explained why and then continued, "There's no law that says things that come in pairs have to be identical." She rocked her head to point out her unmatched earrings. I saw her glance down and wondered if she was going to hold her feet up and show off that her socks didn't match. But she seemed to reconsider and left it at the earrings.

"You can pick your yarn from the bins against the wall. There is a selection of solid colors and the self-striping yarn in different color-ways."

"And be sure to take one of the tote bags to keep your project in," I said, pointing to the pile of blood-red bags with *Yarn2Go* on the front. "They are already packed with a set of needles and a sheet with directions, along with instructions on the basics of knitting." I added that they could help themselves to the refreshments.

Crystal and I watched with interest to see who would pick the self-striping yarn. Victor Ackroyd picked the multicolored yarn, but his wife Leslie chose a rust-colored solid. Sandra Elliott seemed interested in making a pair that would blend but not match and chose one of the cakes of yarn. She picked out a toast-brown solid for Bruce.

Rose Wilburn was enamored with the cakes of yarn and the way all the colors were visible from the top. She took some pictures, but then opted for a rose-colored solid.

"I'm just a beginner," Milton Carruthers said. "I'll stick to what seems the easiest." He grabbed a skein of loden-green yarn. Jenn Van Ness let her daughter do the choosing and she came back with cream-colored yarn for both of them. Mary Smith seemed indifferent about the whole thing and appeared to grab a random skein of the solid yarn.

Madeleine waited until the end and gave Crystal a flash of her eyebrows as she picked one of the cakes of yarn in shades of blue. "Mrs. Maple is always up for something adventurous."

They all grabbed drinks and cookies along with the yarn supplies and came back to the table. Crystal demonstrated casting on the stitches. Those who knew how to knit did it with ease, but she had to give Milton Carruthers a private lesson. Sandra Elliott did the same with her husband and hardly seemed to enjoy doing it. In the end, Crystal and Sandra took the easy way out and cast on the stitches along with knitting the first couple of rows before turning it over to the two men.

Crystal did a demonstration of the pattern of knit and purl stitches that created the ribbed look and watched as the newbies struggled through the first row.

I stayed as an observer, glad to turn everything over to Crystal for a while. It had been *go go go* and I hadn't had a chance to process anything of what I'd seen or what had happened. I had gotten myself a cup of coffee and was just beginning to go over the morning so far, when any chance for my solitary thoughts was lost.

It started when someone brought up the chalk outline and scattered clues in the next room. "I agree with whoever said finding out what happened to the real corpse is a lot more interesting than dealing with a fake murder," Milton Carruthers said. "We could use our sleuthing skills to figure out what happened and present it to the rumpled detective. It's always so much fun when amateurs show up the professionals."

"I like that idea," Leslie Ackroyd said. "It would make such an interesting story to share with our Stitch and Sip buddies."

I was getting tenser and tenser as each of them spoke. Even though I agreed with them. It was much more interesting to solve a real crime rather than a faked one and I had my own secret pleasure of besting Lieutenant Borgnine in the past, but having the group get in the middle of the lieutenant's investigation could be trouble. He could arrest them for interfering. Maybe not Madeleine, since she was such a big deal in the small town, but certainly the others. I could just imagine what kind of review someone would leave on my Facebook feed if they ended up spending the weekend in jail.

"We really should leave it to the professionals," I said.

Crystal was clearly staying out of it, but Madeleine shook her head as she looked at me. "But Casey, that's not what you've done before. How many times now have you been the one to solve a real crime around here. I agree with the others, as Mrs. Maple, the lead detective, I say we go for it."

Madeleine was certainly full of surprises. One minute she was letting her sister bully her and then she was anxious to take the reins and play sleuth. I really didn't think that Lieutenant Borgnine would arrest her, but who knew for sure. After a moment's thought, I acknowledged there seemed to be no way to talk her, or the group, out of getting involved. The only alternative seemed for me to work with them and somehow keep them all out of Lieutenant Borgnine's way.

I stood up to address the group. "Okay, here is what we'll do. As Madeleine, I mean Mrs. Maple, said, I have some experience in solving some crimes. I was an assistant private detective before I came to Cadbury." They all nodded with admiration before I continued. "I will see what I can find out and then we can all discuss it. But we need to keep all our observations to the group."

"I get it. The cop in the wrinkled jacket could threaten to arrest us for interfering with or obstructing the investigation," Rose Wilburn said. "I heard that on one of the true crime podcasts I listened to." She seemed more animated as she glanced at the others, as if it would be somehow titillating to have someone slip handcuffs on her.

"We don't want that to happen, do we?" I said, stopping at each one's face until I got a nod that they agreed.

"I hate to interrupt," Crystal said, holding up her arm with her watch, "but we need to stop now." The experienced knitters knew to make sure they finished a row before they stopped and to mark down where they left off, but she had to help Milton. And then step in with Bruce because Sandra was shaking her head and looking away from him, clearly out of patience. In addition to being an Olympic-level complainer, Bruce was also stubborn about taking help, particularly from his wife. Crystal cringed when she looked at the rows he'd done, and under the guise of straightening his work, ripped out a couple of rows and redid them at warp speed before handing it back.

The bell outside the Sea Foam dining hall was ringing, announcing lunch as everyone filed out of the meeting room. I stuck with them until we got to the center of the grounds and sent them off to their meal. I paused just long enough to wave to Crystal as she went to her car, and then I rushed up the driveway and across the street. I had work to do.

Chapter 15

I wanted to get right to it, but Julius insisted on a snack and some attention. I went through the whole stink fish thing quickly and spent a few minutes using a glove that worked like a brush on his black fur while he pressed against it and purred loudly.

"You good?" I said, looking at the cat as I pulled off the wad of black hair. I took his silence as a yes and went to give my cell phone a quick survey. There was a text from my mother saying she'd left several messages on my landline and needed to hear from me to be sure I was all right.

I grabbed the landline and ignored the beeping to let me know of her messages and punched in a number. The ringing seemed to go on forever and I was preparing to leave a voicemail when Frank answered.

"Feldstein, I'm tailing somebody, so if you're calling to tell me about the knitters, can we do it later?"

"Not exactly," I said. "Time is an issue."

I heard Frank let out his breath. "Okay, I'm putting you on speaker. The mark just went into a motel room. And now I have to wait for his girlfriend to show." There was a pause and I heard the rustle of paper. I knew that Frank always brought along a sub sandwich when he expected to have to wait around watching people cheat on their spouses or con insurance companies. There was an abrupt change of sounds as he muttered that the girlfriend was knocking on the door. "Got it, you cheating son of a B," he said with triumph. "Photos of him and his babe in the bag, so I'm all yours now. Last I heard you were getting ready for your retreat group to solve a fake murder. What happened?"

As soon as he heard there was an actual corpse, he let out an *aha* sort of noise. "Didn't I warn you about that. I bet that rumpled cop is on your case."

"Lieutenant Borgnine did make a comment about not getting

involved with an implied threat it could cause problems," I said. "I can deal with that. It's that the group wants to throw off the fake murder and as they put it, use their skills on solving the real one and showing up Borgnine." I let out a mirthless chuckle. "He didn't make the best impression on them and they're all about podcasts and TV shows where the amateurs outshine the cops."

"Got it," Frank said. There was just the hint of impatience in his voice and I knew I better get to the point fast.

"I need to get information on the dead guy and maybe some others. You have access to all those information sites . . ."

"I pay for them," Frank said.

"I'll send you a box of cookies," I said. "I made sandwich cookies with real buttercream inside."

Frank let out an *mmm* sound at the description. "Okay, Feldstein, I guess I could take that as payment. So, what do you need?"

The deceased's name is Gary Moser. He seems about in his fifties and was at Vista Del Mar alone, though he seemed on the prowl. Maybe he didn't realize what kind of place it is."

"Got it. He was looking for short-term love in the wrong sort of place. It would help if you had some more information about him, like where he was from and if his middle name started with a Z," Frank said with a chortle.

"It's all I know for now. See what you can do with that. And I'd like to find out about a woman who seemed unhappy with his attention."

"I'll need a little more than that, like at least a name," Frank said.

"Well, duh," I said with a laugh. "I'll check with my source about her and see if I can get some more details on the dead guy to narrow it down since you'll probably come up with a list of Gary Mosers." I chuckled to myself, thinking that Cloris would probably like being referred to as my source.

"I'll check on the guy when I get back to my computer and give you a call," Frank said. "When did you say you'd put those cookies in the mail?"

"Monday, I promise," I said before trying to pin him down for a specific time for the call.

"That's right. No cell or WiFi at the haunted hotel. One of these days, I have to come out there and see it for myself. I like to see the faces that go along with all those names you're giving me all the time."

"I could send you pictures," I said and he laughed.

"Not the same as seeing them in 3-D." He went back to figuring out a time I would be at my place and he would be available. "It's Friday night," Frank said. "I got plans."

I still didn't know much about his personal life beyond that he had a cat he'd rescued named Mittens. And that I was pretty sure there was no Mrs. Frank. With the two-hour difference in time and my schedule with the group, we finally nailed down a time and hung up.

I was getting ready to go back, hoping to catch the last of lunch. The oatmeal had long since worn off and I could only eat so many cookies as a meal. I was halfway to the backdoor when I saw Sammy looking through the glass portion of it. His face lit up when he saw me and I motioned for him to come in.

He looked around as if he was worried about being seen, in a melodramatic joking sort of way, before he came inside.

"So has your crew figured out who did me in yet?" he said with a merry expression. "They sure made it tough for me to keep playing dead. Someone who bent close had horrible breath and then I thought I was going to sneeze." He was so breezy in his manner, there was no way he knew about the latest incident.

His expression changed as soon as he heard there was a real corpse. I described the guy and Sammy nodded with recognition. "Didn't he crash the reception? I saw him go in when I was waiting in the wings to do my thing."

"You're right," I said. "He didn't really crash it, though. He came with one of my people, like it was a date or something. But then he didn't stay." I took a moment to compare Mary Smith to the younger woman I'd seen him hit on before. "His taste in women was all over the place."

Sammy shrugged off the comment and went back to talking about his performance. "What did you think of my acting? I thought I did pretty good in those little scenes."

I thought back to his encounters in front of my group and was going to give him kudos and then I remembered the one with Cloris. "You and Cloris seemed to have a moment," I said. "It looked like sparks were flying."

Sammy looked down and swallowed. "I didn't know that it showed." He seemed uncomfortable. "We sort of got carried away with our parts." He got himself a glass of water. "You know I always say you're the only one who gets me." I realized that he thought I was upset by what I'd seen. No matter what he'd said to the contrary, I knew he was still hoping we'd get back together.

"It's okay," I said. "You're single. She's single. You're both good people." I left it hanging and hoped he'd fill in the rest. It was fine with me if they got together. I really meant that even though I felt a slight twinge. I had gotten used to his adoration and wasn't so sure about it going away.

There was an awkward silence after that, which I got out of by seeing the time on the kitchen wall clock. "I'm starving and I want to get to the dining hall before lunch ends. Want to come?"

Sammy laughed. "No way. Your people can't see that I'm living and breathing. The whole plan was that I'd disappear."

"I don't think that is an issue anymore. They're all about the real dead guy now." It was a relief to have the subject changed back to the retreat.

"Wow," he said, surprised. "I thought they'd want to get justice for me. Who's the killer, anyway?" I thought at first that he was being facetious, but he seemed genuinely disappointed.

"To keep it exciting, only Cloris and the designated person knew who was supposed to have done the deed," I said with a shrug.

"And now it just seems like a big waste of ketchup," he said.

Even with what I'd told Sammy, he still didn't want to show that he was actually alive to the retreat group and join me for lunch. I was sure he was hoping they'd reconsider and want to find out who had done him in. Nothing more was said about Cloris, and I decided it was none of my business and up to them if anything happened next. He left to go home and I rushed across the street.

I had to hand it to Kevin St. John, once again he had kept it to business as usual despite the fact that there was a body on the second floor of the Sand and Sea building waiting for pickup. *Life goes on* could have been his mantra. Whatever investigating they were doing was completely out of sight of the guests. There had been some grumbling from my group when I explained the whole building was off-limits for the moment and they couldn't go to their rooms. I'd assured them that the investigating would be done efficiently and by afternoon it would be as if nothing had happened. Nobody said anything, but I'm sure we were all thinking the same thought. Maybe for us, but not for the dead guy.

I had to walk through the crowd who were finished with lunch and were on their way to their afternoon activities. The Sea Foam dining hall had the same touches of dark wood and local stone as the other structures, but the dining hall had more windows looking out into the trees and undergrowth. The massive stone fireplace was unlit and most of the round wood tables were empty. The man at the host stand seemed surprised by my arrival and started to say lunch was almost over and to ask for my meal ticket, but then he saw it was me. All I knew about him was his name was Skyler. He waved me in and I started to sprint toward the cafeteria-style line at the back. The kitchen workers were in the process of shutting down, but a woman in a white coat took pity on me and made me a grilled cheese sandwich and gave me the last of the tomato soup. Someone else stuck a bowl of tapioca pudding on my tray.

The dining area was even more empty now, but then I recognized

Mary Smith's blunt-cut white hair. She was sitting alone at one of the tables with an open laptop. When I got closer, I saw that she was typing something.

"Did you find a way to get WiFi?" I said as a joke when I stopped next to her.

"Oh," she said in a panicked voice as she jerked her head in my direction. She caught me glancing toward the computer and snapped it closed. It only took a moment for her to recover and answer my comment. "Ha ha, or should I say LOL? Nope, I'm just cut off from everything like everyone else." She looked at my tray. "You barely made it." Her tone seemed friendly enough but there was undercurrent of unease.

She pushed her chair back just as I was sitting. "Well, I'll leave you to it" She went to collect the computer. She was making an effort to be slow and casual, but there was just enough subtle jerking in her movements to make it clear she was in a hurry to get out of there.

"Don't leave," I said. "I know for a fact there's nothing on the schedule for another hour." I was keeping my tone light. "We've never had a chance to talk one on one. It's always a regret I have for the retreats—not getting a chance to know each of the people."

She apparently saw no way out and gave up trying to leave, though she did slip the computer in the bag hanging on the back of the chair next to her.

I was curious about what she'd been typing and a whole lot more, like how she'd ended up bringing Gary Moser to the reception and what she knew about him, but I couldn't jump right to those topics without seeming strange. I'd have to ease my way in. I took the plates off my tray and put them on the table. I reached for the vacuum pot on the lazy Susan and used it to fill the empty mug that was sitting at my place.

"Refill?" I said, holding the pot over her mug. She nodded and I poured, making a comment on how good the coffee was. Whatever she had felt on guard about seemed to be going away.

"I'm sure glad I got here in time," I said, picking up the sandwich and taking a bite. I tasted the tomato soup and commented on how good it was.

"It was quite a morning. Was that typical for the retreats you put on?" she asked. At first, I thought she was being facetious, but her face was dead serious.

"This whole retreat has been different than what I usually do," I said.

"What exactly happened? I went to get a cup of coffee and when I came back to the Sand and Sea building it seemed like all hell had broken loose." She took a sip of the coffee. "No one really gave details during the workshop other than it seems like somebody died."

I was surprised that she seemed to know so little and was immediately suspicious. Was it true or was she covering something up?

"It was a man named Gary Moser," I said. I watched for her reaction. It was just a slight tell, but she seemed to stiffen when I gave the name. "I think you knew him. He came to the afternoon tea with you."

"He didn't really come with me," she said. "He told me that he'd left something in that room we were using and asked if he could walk in with me so it would look like he was part of the group. I couldn't imagine why that would be a problem so I agreed. He didn't even give me his name," she added quickly. She sat back for a moment while it all sunk in. "I don't have to tell the police that I brought him into the tea, do I? Why would they even want to talk to me since I wasn't in the building when he was found. I didn't even know who died until just now." She seemed a little desperate. "I can't be implicated in a murder." She took a nervous sip of water.

"Do you think our group is really going to investigate it? Do you think any of them saw me with *him*? You won't say anything, will you?" she pleaded.

I thought it over for a moment and came up with a solution. "It's up to you what you tell Lieutenant Borgnine. But all I know is that he came in for a few minutes and left."

Really, if I thought about it, Gary Moser's pattern seemed to be that he got himself in situations where he didn't belong. First there was the woman who told him to back off, then he'd been hanging around me when I was checking everyone in, and finally his showing up at the afternoon tea. It could have been that he was just interested in the food. It did seem he'd eaten and run. I wasn't sure how his peeking in the Sand and Sea lobby window fit in, but maybe he was a Peeping Tom.

She was calmed by what I said but she still appeared concerned. "I heard all that talk how you used to be an assistant PI and that you were going to help the group follow some clues. Is it really true that you have caught some killers?"

Something in the way she was asking made me uncomfortable and I tried to downplay what I'd done in the past and my plans for the weekend. "My only concern is our retreat group and that they have a satisfactory weekend and they don't get into trouble with Lieutenant Borgnine."

"So, finding out who killed him isn't really a priority?" she asked. I could tell that she wanted me to say she was correct and I wasn't going to play sleuth, so I nodded in agreement. The truth was, it wasn't my top priority. I'd only gotten interested when Madeleine and the rest of them had insisted they wanted to ditch what happened to Sammy and turn their detective skills on what happened to Gary Moser. My biggest concern was keeping them all out of trouble.

I finished off the last of the sandwich and soup and put my dishes along with hers on the tray. I got up to carry them to the busing station. By now even the host was gone and the door to the cafeteria area was closed. We walked outside into a cool afternoon even though by the look of the sky it could have still been morning. A gust of damp wind ruffled my jacket and I went to zip it. I was sticking to the Katherine Hepburn look of loose slacks and a shirt, but while the sweater complimented the outfit, it was like a sieve when it came to the brisk air. The black nubby fleece jacket might not exactly fit the some-other-time look, but it made up for it in warmth.

She said something about going for a walk to clear her head. I assumed she'd want to drop the computer off and reminded her that the whole Sand and Sea building was still off-limits. "But you can leave it behind the counter in the Lodge," I said. I offered to do it for her, but she put her hand protectively over the bag. "I'll drop it off myself," she said.

I walked with her and brought her up to the counter. She did a little double take when she saw Kevin St. John talking to a couple who had just come in. "El Bosso," she said in a mixture of awe and concern from having seen him in the little scenes.

Cloris was behind the counter and it seemed that Mary had forgotten that the tall assistant manager was also one of the suspects in Sammy's demise and immediately responded to her friendliness when she asked what we needed.

Cloris picked up on Mary's concern about the computer bag and assured her it would be in a separate vault and she gave Mary the key. I wondered if Mary was aware that being nice and friendly didn't exclude someone from being a killer. It just made you want it not to be true.

As soon as Mary was gone, Cloris's smile faded a little and she started apologizing for everything. "If only I hadn't moved him to Sand and Sea, it wouldn't have interfered with your retreat," she said. "But he was insistent."

Chapter 16

The Lodge was quiet for the moment. In the middle of the afternoon guests were either off on excursions or in a meeting room doing something connected to the group they were there with. Or like my group, with free time.

"I was going to get a cup of coffee," Cloris said. "Want to join me?"

"That would be great," I said. "I'd like to talk to you about what happened this morning." We went into the café and Bob poured us cups of the brew of the day. A few of the tables were taken, and even though the one in the corner would have given us some privacy, I suggested we take our drinks outside.

We crossed over to the grassy area across from the Lodge. It was the only area that had actual tall green grass because it got the moist wind that blew off the water. We took one of the benches along the edge and had enough privacy that we could have yelled to each other and nobody would have heard us.

I got right to it and asked Cloris what she knew about what had happened to Gary Moser.

"I only got bits and pieces, but it seems like he was electrocuted with a hair dryer. An extension cord was plugged in somewhere in the room, and it looked like he must have been in the shower and had the hair dryer going or something like that," she said with a shrug.

"And he fell out of the shower taking the plastic curtain with him. The bathrooms are so tiny and he seemed like a pretty big man," I said. "I only got a glance before we were rushed out of there, but that's what I saw." Even though where we were sitting seemed private, I checked the area before I continued. "Did the lieutenant say anything about it being murder or an accident?" Borgnine had made a point not to commit what it was to my group, but I was sure his gut had already kicked in and he'd decided what it was even if it wouldn't be official until the medical examiner decided.

"I heard him tell Mr. St. John that he thought it was murder because no man would be stupid enough to be so concerned about styling his hair that he picked up an appliance while standing in the shower." She gave me a knowing look. "I concur. Not about the stupidity part. Men can be just as vain as women about their hair, but not that guy. He seemed pretty unconcerned with his appearance. And it wasn't like he had a lot of hair to work with."

"What about the guy?" I asked. "What do you know about him?"

"Not much other than his name and that he gave an address in Santa Clara. And he hung around the Lodge a lot staring at people."

"Did you notice him trying to pick up women?" I asked.

"Maybe that's why he was staring," she said with a shrug.

"There was a woman in sweats and a baseball cap that he seemed to be hitting on the other night. She told him to get lost. Do you know anything about her?"

"I'd need a little more description than that." She nodded toward a group of people who had just stepped off the boardwalk and were passing by us. The three of them were wearing sweat outfits and baseball caps. "Except for your group, it seems like it's either sweats, cargo pants or jeans."

"I guess it is a little generic," I said. "If I see her again, I'll point her out."

She looked into her cup and saw that it was almost empty. "Time to go back," she said, taking the last sip. There was a last thing I wanted to ask her.

"Before you go," I said as she flattened the empty cup. "I'm a little suspicious about a woman in my group. She's the one who just left her computer. She says her name is Mary Smith." I looked at Cloris with a knowing look. "But really, Mary Smith? It sounds a little fake to me. Did you happen see any ID when you checked her in?"

"We only ask for ID if the name on their credit card doesn't match the name they want to register with. I do remember her. Instead of giving us a credit card to have on file, she gave a deposit of cash, which is unusual. But it could be her real name. The reason it sounds fake is because it is such a common name, which means there must be a lot of real Mary Smiths running around."

"Good point," I said. We both got up to leave.

No matter what Cloris said about there probably being a lot of real Mary Smiths, I wasn't sold that the one in my group was one of them. Even Cloris had said leaving a cash deposit was unusual. It seemed like she was hiding something. I remembered that Kevin St. John had found her wandering in the business area and she'd opened the envelope of clues early, and that didn't even consider her bringing Gary Moser to the tea. I figured it was pretty useless to give her name to Frank. But I did wonder about the woman I'd seen the dead guy try to pick up. I'd have to keep on the lookout for her and hopefully get a name from Cloris. The only thing I had found out was that Gary Moser came from Santa Clara, which might be enough to separate him from the herd if Frank came up with a list of people with the name.

There was no time to go home and call Frank with the news that Gary Moser was from Santa Clara, so I'd have to wait for our call later in the day. I wanted to get to the meeting room early to check on everything. I chided myself for being so anxious to go across the street and call Frank that morning that I'd just rushed out and left everything as it was. Normally, I would have stayed after the group left and cleared up the used paper cups left around and gathered any snippets of yarn on the table. The air pots would have been taken back to Cloris with a reminder of the afternoon workshop. I'd even forgotten to mention it when I just saw her.

Despite all, she was on top of things with no reminder. It was clear the room had been serviced. The chairs were all pushed into the table. The used cups and bits of yarn were all gone, and when I looked at the two air pots on the counter, I was confident they had been refilled.

I left my things on the same chair I'd used earlier. It was a funny thing, but it seemed true for every retreat. Once everyone picked a spot, they returned to it the whole weekend as though the chair had been assigned.

I went to check the crime scene. Despite what some of them had said about abandoning the game of clues we'd set up, I wanted to make sure everything was in order in case there were others who were still interested in figuring out who did in Sammy.

The chalk outline was still okay, as were the clues that had been spread around it. Only one piece of paper with a footprint had drifted across the room. The pool of ketchup had turned a rust brown with bits of dried-up stuff in it.

"So this is the famous crime scene," a voice behind me said. Lieutenant Borgnine stopped next to me and looked at the drying ketchup. "How was this supposed to work?"

"We set it up so that Sammy had some scenes with various people here to set up the drama. I took the group off the grounds and the murder scene was set up with Sammy sprawled on the ground." I pointed to the papers on the ground. "Those are clues. The group could work together or on their own to follow the clues and 'question' the suspects." I shrugged. "And in the middle of it all, they'd have some yarn events."

"You ought to make sure they work together, because if someone goes rogue and figures it out first, it would be ruined for the others," the gruff cop said. "And I'd get rid of that ketchup if I were you."

"It's the first time I've done anything like this," I said. "There are kinks to be worked out."

"First time?" he said in a wary tone. "Does that mean there are going to be more?"

"It's not my call. This was all Madeleine Delacorte's—" I searched for the right word. *Suggestion* was too weak and *command* too strong. I put up my hands. "It just depends on what she wants."

Borgnine didn't look happy with my answer. He knew he could try to bully me, but not Madeleine. The Delacortes were the police department's purse. They were the ones who donated money when Cadbury PD needed a new cruiser or some updated equipment. They were behind the pancake breakfast fundraiser and even attended, though it was closer to making an appearance. So, if Madeleine wanted more weekends of being Mrs. Maple, he couldn't stand in the way.

"I'm assuming you're here about something else," I said, leading him out of the larger room with the crime scene to the smaller one set up for us. Cory was on his way out.

"I added some more wood to the fire," the teenager said. "What's happening with Sammy's murder? Isn't somebody supposed to question me and see if my shoe print matches the one at the crime scene?"

Lieutenant Borgnine closed his eyes with frustration. It had been enough when it was just the Delacorte sisters who got special treatment. But now he had to treat Cory with consideration too, since he was part of the Delacorte family. "Your great-great-aunts should be proud of you. The way you are starting at the bottom here at Vista Del Mar."

Cory smiled at the praise, but it was really unnecessary, as was any special treatment from the cop. Cory loved Vista Del Mar and did even the lowliest job with enthusiasm.

"I'll be ready if the retreat people come," he said, slinging the bag that had carried the wood over his shoulder. "And I remember that you said we could lie."

Borgnine looked at me and shook his head. "You told the suspects that they could lie?"

"It's just a game," I said, and I didn't want it to be too easy.

With Cory gone, Borgnine finally got to the point of why he was there. "This isn't the first time we've been through this," he said with regret in his voice. "So you know the drill. I need to get statements from all of your people. I'd appreciate it if you would encourage them to be helpful." He waited to get a nod from me. "But before we get to them, I need one from you." He had a clipboard with forms and a pen.

"You probably know all about it by now," I said. "Who the deceased is and that the cause of death was murder."

"Ms. Feldstein, I know that you know that is to be determined by the medical examiner."

"You're calling me Ms. Feldstein again," I said in surprise.

"Yes, since we're in a professional setting," he said. I guessed he only called me Casey when it had to do with my muffins and his adoration of them and all that I baked. But even then, I called him by his title. He'd made it clear he didn't want to be called Theo or Theodore by me ever.

"Can we get to this?" He had his pen in his hand and was already filling in the top information, like my name and such.

"But you must have a gut feeling," I said, going back to the cause of death.

"If I did, which I don't, I wouldn't share it with any civilians." His eyes went to the refreshment setup and I offered to get him a coffee and some cookies. I knew that sweets were the direct route to get through all the gruffness.

His eyes lit up when he saw the sandwich cookies. "Please don't tell Mrs. Borgnine. She's anti-cookies these days. Make the coffee black," he said. "It'll balance everything off."

He took a bite of the double butter cookies with pink buttercream icing in between. He was speechless, but his expression said it all as he closed his eyes again, but this time with pleasure.

He had a hard time getting back to his tough demeanor, but he did. "I know you're pretty observant, so if you could tell me what you saw, but please leave out your opinion of what happened."

I set up the scene, saying I'd come to gather up my group and we all heard a scream coming from the second floor. "The door was open to one of the rooms and a housekeeping cart was in the hall. I got caught with some people trying to squeeze through the door at the same time. The housekeeper was standing near to the door to the bathroom. When we came up behind her, I saw a man laying half out of the shower. There was something black on the floor touching him. It was connected to one of those heavy-duty orange extension cords.

That's really all I saw. Kevin St. John rushed in and got us all out of there." I looked at him and smiled. "That's it. Just the facts with no editorializing from me."

"Just to be clear, the deceased wasn't one of your retreat people?" he asked when I'd finished. I answered with a shake of my head. "Do you know what his profession was?" I shook my head again. It was the truth for now, but I hoped I'd know that and more after I talked to Frank.

He seemed almost disappointed with the brief recap I'd given him. Since he just wanted the facts, I didn't include anything about my encounters with Gary Moser or that he seemed on the prowl.

"Okay, then," he said, clicking the point off of his pen. He got up and I saw him glance at the tin of cookies and offered him another.

He took it with a thank-you and made a move to the door. "I'll be on the bench outside. If you could send your people out one at a time." He gave me one of his scolding nods. "And please don't tell them they can lie."

Chapter 17

"Sorry I'm late," Crystal said, rushing in. "I went to the store in the time between workshops and a tourist bus unloaded in front of the store. It was a woman's group from San Jose who'd stopped on their way to go whale watching. A lot of them were knitters and had to come in because Cadbury Yarn was so adorable." She paused as the word she'd used sunk in. "I better not let the town council hear that word. They'd probably show up at the store and demand that we de-adorablize it."

I started to laugh at the concept. "What would be so terrible if they bent a little. People come here from around the world because of the natural beauty of the cypress trees and the coastline. Would it be so terrible to have a saltwater taffy shop and a ye olde T-shirt shop that sold shirts that said *I Had a Whale of a Time in Cadbury by the Sea?*"

"I'm with you," she said. "But the powers that be are stuck in their way," Crystal said as she began to unload her tote bag with samples of the hand warmers in different stages of being made.

We hadn't had time to talk before about what happened to Gary Moser and I quickly brought her up to speed. I described him and said that he'd been at Vista Del Mar before my group arrived. "Did you see him?" I asked. "Or more to the point, did he come on to you?" With her colorful attire, he would have surely noticed her when she came to pick Cory up.

"Nope, no blah-looking guy with colorless brown hair made a move on me," she said with a laugh. "I might have gone for it. Aside from that musician Robert I told you about, my social life is a big zero."

She started to ask me if there was anything she should know about my group.

"It's turned into the inmates running the asylum. They decided to chuck finding Sammy's killer in favor of investigating the real thing. Lieutenant Borgnine has already warned me to keep them out of it."

"What about Madeleine?" she asked.

"She seems to be right there with them," I said. I heard someone coming down the path and looked to the door just as Madeleine came in and looked around.

"I'm here, I'm here," Madeleine said, looking at the empty table. "I thought I was late. Cora showed up and insisted I had to go to a luncheon with her. It was for a fundraiser for the animal shelter, and even though we were never allowed to have a pet, I have a soft spot for dogs. When we used to have a pet shop in town, there was a poodle in the window that I really wanted. The point of the luncheon was to add to the storefront that has cats for adoption and make one for dogs." She looked down at her tweed suit. "Cora had a fit that I showed up in this, but everybody was excited to hear about me being Mrs. Maple and our mystery weekend. And when they heard there was a real death and we were on the case, they were fascinated."

I traded glances with Crystal and she gave me a knowing nod. The group started to file in just then. They were all talking and animated as I watched them come in. Something seemed off with Victor Ackroyd, and then I saw that he had his walking stick tucked under his arm. I checked his gait and there wasn't even a limp. Leslie must have noticed me staring and she gave his arm a nudge. Instantly, he started to limp and even appeared to catch himself by grabbing a chair as he lowered the walking stick. Mary Smith had her computer bag back and appeared to avoid my eye. I almost didn't recognize Jenn Van Ness with her frizzy hair pulled into a topknot. Emily was right behind her and rushed ahead to pull out the chair for her mother.

"Please, stop treating me like I'm helpless," Jenn said in a sharp tone. Everyone looked at her and she quickly apologized. "I know you mean the best," the mother said.

Milton Carruthers was carrying a book and he handed it off to Leslie Ackroyd. "I personalized it as you requested." He turned to the rest of them. "There are still a few copies in the gift shop, if anyone is interested."

Rose Wilburn walked in alone and found the chair she'd used before. She saw the knitted pieces on the table and started arranging them and taking photos with her phone. Sandra Elliott was holding up the rear. Her whole demeanor had changed and she seemed relaxed.

"Bruce decided to sit this one out," she said in a happy tone. I remembered that she had mentioned how going to her knitting and crochet group had been a night out away from his complaining. I guessed she was looking at the workshop that way. My worry was that he was off investigating on his own.

Before they got too situated, I broke the news about Lieutenant Borgnine being ready to take their statements. I did as he asked and explained it wasn't anything to get uptight about and that he probably just wanted to hear what they'd seen and heard regarding the man on the second floor.

"I wasn't there," Mary Smith called out. "I went to get coffee. You were all rushing out when I came back to the building."

"Then tell that to the lieutenant," I said. She still had a worried look and I was sure it was related to our earlier conversation. "For all of you, just tell him what you know to the best of your recollection. He's not a big-city cop who is going to shut you in a tiny brightly lit room and interrogate you. He put all that behind him when he came here. He's sitting outside on a bench."

"Is the victim the guy who showed up at the afternoon tea?" Milton said.

Mary Smith let out a gasp and then caught herself, giving all her attention to the pumpkin-colored skein of yarn and her work in progress. "That's right," I said, feigning surprise. "There was someone who came in for a short time. It could have been him. He must have been looking for something."

"Does anybody know who he is—or was?" Victor Ackroyd said. He had the pad of paper that I'd included in the tote bags on the table in front of him and a pen poised to write. I hoped he wouldn't pull it out when it was his turn to talk to Borgnine. There was a certain arrogance about him and his wife with their stylish clothes and talk about the Stitch and Sip group. I was afraid that he would expect Lieutenant Borgnine to view him as a colleague.

"I'm working on it," I said, hoping to dissuade any of them from trying to do it on their own.

"Maybe the cop will tell us," Rose Wilburn said. "I'll go first and use my feminine wiles to see what I can find out." She made a pouty mouth and strutted in a vamp impression as she crossed the room. She carried it off about as well as I did with my attempts at flirting. There was something very proper about her and a little stiff, which made her femme fatale attempt almost laughable. And would be a waste of time with Borgnine. If she wanted to soften him up, she'd have to bring cookies. I gave her directions to where he was sitting and she went out the door.

Crystal encouraged them to take out their knitting. "We want to do our best to at least finish one of the hand warmers while you're here in case you need help sewing up the side." Emily held up hers to show the others she had already completed half the rectangle for one of the fingerless gloves. "I'm a nervous knitter," she said. "Some people eat ice cream when they get tense. It's all needle action with me."

"I suppose it's about what happened this morning. Who would have thought there would be a real murder and we'd have to talk to the police," Mary Smith said.

"It's more about you," Emily said, glancing at her mother. "I just wanted you to enjoy this weekend and get away from it all." Her brow furrowed with concern as she let out a sigh.

Jenn put her arm around her daughter and gave her shoulders a squeeze. "You have to understand that some things follow you wherever you go." She touched her head to her daughter's. "I promise to lighten up for the rest of the weekend."

Sandra Elliott nodded in agreement. "It's hard when you bring the baggage with you." Her gaze moved to the empty chair next to her. "This was supposed to be a chance for us to do something for us together. I really believed that if we got away from all the everyday stuff, it would be like a romantic weekend. We'd be like the *Hart to Hart* couple wrapped up in a mystery." She looked at the empty chair again. "Ha! What's that thing about leopards not changing their spots," she muttered under her breath.

I took her mention of playing a mystery-solving TV couple as a way to bring up Sammy's demise and their responsibility for finding his killer, but that ship seemed to have sailed and all they wanted to talk about was being questioned by Lieutenant Borgnine.

Then they started to do exactly what they weren't supposed to and that was discuss what they'd seen. "You probably should wait until after you give your statements before you share what you remember," I said.

"Of course," Milton Carruthers said. "All the talking amongst ourselves could influence what we think we saw."

"I suppose being a mystery writer, you know things like that," Mary Smith said. "Have you ever been involved with a real crime before this?"

"This is the closest I've come," he said. "But I do a lot of research about cold cases for plot ideas and then create my own solution for them. And tailor it to my park ranger sleuth. I have to figure out something for her cat to do to help solve the crime." He pointed to the book he'd signed for Mary Smith. It was called A *Mountain of Murder* and featured a woman in a ranger's uniform sitting around a campfire with a fluffy white Persian cat and mountains in the background.

Madeleine had been quiet during all this and she seemed to be taking some deep breaths. I pulled her aside. "Are you okay?" I asked, noting her brow was furrowed in concern.

"It's just that I've never dealt with a policeman in this kind of professional situation. I don't know how I'm supposed to act. I've seen those crime dramas where the policeman hammers at the person until they admit their guilt." I had to restrain myself from smiling as I imagined what I thought she was imagining—that somehow

Lieutenant Borgnine would corner her, then hover over her, demanding to know the truth.

"Remember what I said. He's not shutting you in a room. It's outside on a bench. I'm sure he just wants to know things like if you know anything about the victim and what you saw this morning." I shifted my weight. "You didn't know him, did you?"

She suddenly looked even more uncomfortable. "I think he's the one I saw behind the registration counter when the manager was in the main part of the Lodge dealing with that group in the red shirts. I think they're from an insurance company." She realized that wasn't important to the story and got back to the point. "He was looking at something on the computer. It seemed suspicious to me, so I told Mr. St. John."

"What did he do?" I asked.

"Mr. St. John went right back there and talked to him. They worked it out peacefully and Mr. St. John seemed pleased about something. As if they'd made some arrangement." She looked at the others. "I heard someone say he was at our tea. I must have missed that. What was he doing there?" she said.

"I think he crashed the tea and just stayed long enough to have a cup of something and some food," Milton Carruthers said.

She caught herself and had a guilty look. "Oh, dear, we're doing just what we're not supposed to. We're talking things over together." She looked at all of them. "I won't say anything about it. I wouldn't want any of us to get arrested."

"I wouldn't want that to happen either," I said. "Just answer the lieutenant's questions and you'll do fine." I meant it for all of them but I was looking at her.

She must have believed me because when Rose Wilburn returned, Madeleine rushed to the door, volunteering to be next.

I thought of going out and offering the lieutenant some more cookies when the last of my group returned. He was used to questioning suspects, but dealing with a bunch of people who were into playing detective had to be exhausting. Sandra Elliott was the last person to return and she said Lieutenant Borgnine was off to find her husband.

Her lips curved in a big smile. "Let the cop listen to his complaints for a while."

Chapter 18

When the workshop ended, there was free time. After Crystal's comment about at least finishing one of the fingerless gloves during the weekend, a couple of the retreaters wanted to continue on with their knitting. Crystal apologized, but said she had to go. The truth was she was only obligated for the hour.

"We're going to have our own stitch and sip," Leslie Ackroyd said as she and her husband left for the café. I caught a glimpse of their work as they packed it into the red tote bags and was surprised at the quality of their knitting. Or more correctly, lack of quality. The stylish couple had passed themselves off as being experienced knitters. I began to have the feeling that their Stitch and Sip get-togethers were heavier on the sip than the stitch.

Sandra wanted to sit outside and knit. She offered help to anyone who needed it, but there were no takers.

"I just want to go for a walk on the beach," Jenn Van Ness said. "Alone," she said, looking at her daughter. Emily seemed upset with what her mother had said and watched as Jenn walked out the door.

"We were never that close. I really hoped we'd connect more this weekend." She waited until her mother had cleared the area and she went to join Sandra. I felt for her and suddenly felt more kindly about my mother's phone calls.

Mary Smith patted her computer bag and said she was going to the café. The only one who showed any interest in the staged crime scene was Rose Wilburn. But when I followed her to offer some help, she only seemed interested in moving things around and taking pictures. My first instinct was to tell her not to touch anything. But then reality struck and I remembered that it wasn't real.

The only ones who'd decided to stay in the room were Madeleine and Milton Carruthers. She was looking at her work and seemed a little lost. I considered offering to help her. My skills weren't great, but better than hers. I knew that I wasn't supposed to be acting like her ladies' maid or anything, but I felt responsible for her. Even if it was for something like wanting extra towels.

I was about to offer my services when Milton Carruthers slid into the empty seat next to her.

"I'm not sure I could be much help," he said in a friendly voice. "But maybe we can figure it out together. It might be the blind leading the blind, but I'm willing if you are. At least we might have fun."

Madeleine looked at the man next to her as what he'd said sunk in. He wanted to spend time with her and he'd just offered her fun. Instantly, she became girlish and flipped back her hair in a flirtatious manner. I admired how natural it was considering her sheltered life. Maybe it was just a talent you were born with, or you weren't. Milton seemed to be charmed by it and leaned a little closer.

My presence wasn't needed anymore, but I hung around a little longer. It was silly, but I felt like I had to be her chaperone. No surprise, he started talking about his books.

"*Mountains of Murder* is the fourth book in the series. As soon as I decided that Nellie was going to be a knitter, I did a whole lot of research. I have a pretty good idea how to do the basics." He looked at her work. "Like I can tell that you dropped a stitch three rows down." Then he laughed. "But looking at diagrams and videos is not the same as doing it yourself. I remember that there were two choices. You could pick up the dropped stitch or carefully undo your knitting until you reached the missing stitch. I vote for trying to pick up the stitch. If it doesn't work, we can always undo your work to that pesky hole."

He'd laid his work on the table to give all his attention to hers and I checked the quality. After the self-deprecating comments, I expected to see a bunch of uneven stitches that were mostly too tight, but instead the rows he'd done were all at an even tension and looked quite good. He leaned even closer and demonstrated using a crochet hook to take the lost stitch up through the three rows above it and then slipped it back on the needle.

"You're a genius," she said, looking at what he'd done.

"I wouldn't say that," he said. "But it did turn out nicely. Shall we keep going on our projects now? I'll be here if you have another problem."

"That sounds lovely," she said, fluttering her eyelashes. He pulled his chair closer to hers so they could see each other's work, and I was just thinking how sweet it was when he said something that gave me pause.

"So, Mrs. Maple, your real identity is that you are one of the Delacorte sisters. You're like the royal family of Cadbury by the Sea. I bet the view is spectacular from that huge Victorian house," he said.

"You found me out," she said in a playful tone. "I'd appreciate it if it would be our little secret. There's no reason for the rest of the group to know. If they find out that my family owns Vista Del Mar, they'll think I have an advantage over the rest of them. I'm staying in a room just like everybody else's."

Actually, she wasn't. We'd given her a room with more space and changed around the furniture. I didn't want that to get out or the rest of them would be angling for writing desks and a room with more windows. It was kind of abrupt, but I joined their conversation before she started to give away too much.

"Then you two are okay helping each other?" I looked directly at him, wondering about his intentions.

"Yes," he said, answering for both of them. "We'll be fine. You can go off somewhere and put your feet up."

It sounded appealing, but I wanted to ask him more questions. Like how was he so familiar with the Delacorte family? I doubted the other retreaters even knew there was a Delacorte family, let alone that she was part of it. How did he know which Victorian house was theirs? And the biggest question was what were his intentions. I laughed at myself for the choice of words, but I wanted to know if he was just interested in helping her with her knitting, liked her company, or had some other motive. They were worth a lot of money and I'm sure had attracted their share of fortune hunters. I wanted to pull Madeleine aside and give her a little talk on the ways of men. I was getting all worked up feeling I had to look after her. Milton seemed nice enough with the silver hair and neatly trimmed beard, but who knew for sure?

Madeleine was giggling now at some play on words he'd made about yarn in yarns. I'd never seen her like this. In the old days, she'd been like a turtle with its head pulled in. Even when she started wearing denim and seeking out adventures, romance had never come up. I looked hard at Milton hoping that I could project my thoughts. He better not turn out to have an ulterior motive and break her heart or he'd have to deal with me.

I laughed inside at how protective I felt about a woman who was almost old enough to be my grandmother. They were very obviously ignoring me and I finally wrenched myself away.

I stopped in the Lodge to tell Cloris that some of the group was still in the meeting room and to have any cleanup done later. I was also hoping for an update on when my people would have access to their rooms.

At this time of the afternoon, it was quiet in the cavernous room and I thought it was empty. I slid the empty air pots across the wood counter, and in her usual helpful manner, she offered to bring refills to them right away.

"We're having another afternoon tea. I think they can manage without drinks until then, but thank you," I said.

"The thing they teach over and over in the hospitality class I'm taking now is about going the extra mile for the guests."

I was about to remind her that I wasn't really a guest when I noticed her gaze go out into the room. Her expression darkened and her brow furrowed. I turned to see what was causing her concern.

The large space was mostly empty, but a man was standing next to the stone fireplace. I immediately picked up on how different he looked from most of the guests and even my people who had stepped up their style. The outfit was casual but appeared contrived. I was sure the jeans were pricy and the blue T-shirt probably had a high thread count that gave it the silky sheen. He topped it with a brown leather bomber-style jacket that looked so soft, I didn't want to know what it was made of.

His short graying hair was styled in a trendy cut. To me, his whole look shouted, *I'm older, but contemporary—and very wealthy.* There was nothing about him that seemed menacing and I wondered at Cloris's reaction. She continued to stare at him like a pointer dog who'd discovered a fallen bird as I asked about him.

"He came in here yesterday and said he was looking for someone. He showed me a photograph of a woman. She looked a little familiar, but not enough that I recognized her. He wanted to know if she was a guest. When I told him that we had a policy that we didn't give out any information about guests, he got agitated and slid a hundred-dollar bill across the counter, expecting that would change the rules. When I persisted, he demanded to see the manager and I gladly turned him over to Mr. St. John, who I'm sure said the same things." She shook her head with concern. "What's he doing back here?"

The man had settled on one of the couches in the seating area around the fireplace and seemed more interested in a couple that had come in than Cloris. He was clearly trying to get a better look at them. And then his attention moved to a woman who was checking out the row of phone booths.

"I would say that he's decided to see if he can find the woman on his own," I said, which only riled Cloris more.

We were both watching the man focus on another woman who'd come out of the café. The door on the deck side of the room opened and a woman in sweats and a baseball cap stopped halfway inside and scanned the room. When her gaze neared the man, she froze.

I nudged Cloris and gestured with my shoulder. Cloris had barely gotten a look at her when she slipped back out and closed the door silently. I had a delayed reaction and suddenly realized she was the woman I'd seen have the encounter with Gary Moser. He had seemed to be hitting on her and she basically had told him to get lost. I wanted to ask Cloris if she knew the woman's name, but Cloris was too intent on the man.

Finally, she came from behind the registration counter and approached him. I wondered if I should follow her as moral support, but decided to stay by the counter ready to help her if she needed it.

"I told you that we don't give out information about our guests," she said in a sharp tone.

"I got that," he said. "But this is a public space, right?" His voice was calm, but there was something threatening about him. "I'm just checking out this place in case I decide I want to stay here."

Cloris seemed concerned. "I know what you're doing," she said. "You can't sit here and spy on people staying here. It's true that it's a public space, but we don't allow loitering by non-guests."

His demeanor changed as he erupted in anger. "Who do you think you are, telling me what I can't do," he sputtered. "Well then, you just tell her she gets nada when I catch her shacked up with someone. I know that's why she came to a place like this that's cut off from the world." He seemed like a man used to winning and it was hard for him to capitulate to Cloris's will. But he also must have realized that he had no choice. He smacked the leather couch with such force I thought he might have made a hole in it, then he finally went to the door.

"That's his," Cloris said, pointing to a yellow sports car with bat wing doors. We both watched as he had a little trouble getting in the car.

"It has to be tough to be able to afford the toys but have a hard time playing with them," Cloris said.

"Did they teach diplomacy in your hospitality class too?" I asked. She nodded with a smile. "I'm just sorry I couldn't have kept our exchange from the earshot of the guests. No wonder that woman changed her mind about coming in. Who knew what he was going to do?"

"Do you know her name?"

"Technically, I probably shouldn't tell you," she said with a smile as she came back around the counter and started scrolling through the computer. "I have this bizarre memory. I don't remember names offhand, but I do remember room numbers. She's in room 201 in Sand and Sea." She looked at the screen. "And her name is Brook Tanner and she's from Palo Alto. We have a real lot of people this weekend from that whole area around Santa Clara and San Jose. But then we always get a lot of guests from Silicon Valley."

"What do you know about her?" I asked.

"That falls under the discretion thing. All I know is that she's been coming here periodically for the past couple of years." She looked at the computer screen. It seems like she's always checked into a room alone and hung out here most of the time. I shouldn't say this, but I wondered if she was meeting someone here."

"You realize she was staying down the hall from the guy who died," I said.

"I'd forgotten about that," she said.

"Are you going to tell Lieutenant Borgnine?" I asked.

"I'm sure he'll figure it out on his own. I'm doing my best to stay uninvolved. I'm sticking to just giving information like where the orange extension cord came from."

"And?" I said, prompting her to tell me.

"There's a closet for the housekeepers on the second floor with vacuum cleaners and such, including the heavy-duty extension cord."

We discussed who had access to it, which was everyone since there was no lock on the door. Our conversation was ended when a couple came up to the counter and wanted to check in.

At the last minute I remembered to ask her if the cops had taken down the yellow tape blocking the entrance to the Sand and Sea building.

She excused herself from the couple and lowered her voice. She hardly wanted the couple checking in to hear there was a crime scene.

"It's all clear," she said. "Cadbury PD has been very good about trying not to disrupt everything. I think your people are the only ones who know anything happened and that's just because they were staying in that building."

"That's great news. I'll let everyone know. Then it's home to make some lemon bars for the afternoon tea."

Cloris glanced at the couple waiting for her help and gestured that she'd be with them momentarily. "That woman who was here before— Brook Tanner. She's the whole reason we couldn't give your group the whole building. She always stays in that building and had reserved her room before you had even publicized your retreat."

I had started to back away and stopped. "Didn't you say that Gary Moser insisted on changing his room to the Sand and Sea building after he got here?" I said and she nodded.

Was it a coincidence they were both in that building or something more?

Chapter 19

"See, no bogey men," I said to Emily Van Ness and Rose Wilburn as I took them inside the Sand and Sea building. They followed me hesitantly, looking around the empty lobby. A fire was crackling in the fireplace. The statue of the Maltese Falcon appeared to be gazing over the empty room. All seemed normal.

I had made the rounds and found as many of my people as I could and told them that the building had been reopened. The two who were with me had seemed uneasy about going inside and I'd offered to accompany them. I figured that once they went in there, the rest of the group wouldn't have a problem.

I was about to leave when some noise coming from the second floor made us all freeze and turn back to the staircase. I think we all expected to see a ghost or zombie version of the deceased. There was a collective sigh of relief when Brook Tanner came down the stairs followed by Cory, who was helping with her luggage. She was dressed in a wine-colored sweat outfit, still with the baseball cap. There was so much I would have liked to ask her, but she walked past us without so much as a nod. It was the teen who was acting as a porter this time who explained she was moving to a room in the Gulls building.

Rose and Emily seemed panicked and I assured them that the upstairs was empty. I didn't want to specifically say that if the building was reopened, it meant that Gary Moser's body was gone. They said something about moving to another building, but I explained there wasn't another group of rooms available.

"Once we have the afternoon tea and get back to the schedule, nobody will even think about the second floor," I said in a bright voice. *Or that was my hope.* I explained I had to bake something for the tea and distracted their thoughts by describing the lemon bars. When I left them, they were sitting together in the lobby working on the hand warmers.

It was a relief to walk up my driveway and then a shock when I walked in my kitchen and there was someone standing at the sink. It only took a moment for me to see the jeans and blue T-shirt and recognize it was Dane. Once I got over the surprise, I realized he was wearing almost the exact outfit as the man I'd seen at Vista Del Mar but without the leather jacket. It was funny how the same outfit had such a different appearance. Dane's jeans were faded from wear and hugged his body, showing off what great shape he was in. All the jogging and karate served him well. He turned and saw me staring at his pants.

"What?" he said with a smile. "Did I sit in some spaghetti sauce or something?"

"No, I was just comparing your jeans to a rich guy's I saw at Vista Del Mar."

"So, then you were probably thinking how much better I look in mine," he said, doing a twirl. Dane was a little cocky, but he managed to temper it with humor, so he didn't come off as conceited or full of himself. "Who was the guy? One of your retreaters?" he asked.

"Thank heavens, he's not," I said and told him about his encounter with Cloris. It was then that the obvious struck me and I wanted to hit my forehead with a how-could-I-have-missed-it move. Brook Tanner hadn't just backed away to avoid the confrontation between Cloris and the man in the leather jacket. "That woman is the one he's looking for," I said cryptically.

"Is this connected to what happened this morning?" he asked.

"Maybe," I said before his question sunk in. "Then you know all about it?" I started to get excited, thinking I'd get the inside dope.

"I heard a few details," he said, shrugging in a noncommittal manner and turning back to the sink. "I just came by to pick up my plate," he said, pointing out that it was sitting in the sink. "I'm assuming the food met with your approval." I knew what he was doing. It was all about changing the subject and I let it go for the moment.

"I was so ravenous when I got home that I inhaled spaghetti and really only tasted it at the end."

"You certainly are a member of the clean plate club," he said with a laugh as he held up the plate, so clear of food it looked like it had already been washed. "You always joke my sauce is so good you want to lick the plate. Looks like this time you did. Sorry I missed it," he said with a suggestive wiggle of his eyebrows and a grin.

"Sorry to disappoint. There was no sensuous tongue action, I used a piece of bread."

He turned on the water and began to wash off the plate. "When I finish this, I'll take care of Julius's snack." The cat was already moving around his ankles.

"I know what you're doing," I said. "You don't want to talk about what happened to Gary Moser."

"Caught me," he said with a sheepish expression. "I don't know much," he said. "And I'm not supposed to tell you."

I thought of Madeleine's flirting and figured if she could do it, maybe I could pull it off this time. "But you're not really going to listen to Lieutenant Borgnine, are you?" I was using a breathy Marilyn Monroe impression I thought would sound seductive. Thinking of what Madeleine had done with her eyelashes, I attempted to copy it, though it would have worked better if I was wearing mascara. I made the mistake of looking at Dane for his reaction. He was trying to hold it in, but he busted out in a laugh.

"Thank you very much for that. There is nothing like a good laugh to get rid of the stress of the day." When he looked at me, he noticed that I wasn't laughing.

"Oh, no, you were making a serious attempt," he said. "I'm sorry for laughing. You get an A for effort." He put down the dish and stepped over the black cat and gave me a hug.

"Caught me," I said. "I was only sort of serious." I told him about Madeleine and how she'd pulled off flirting.

"Madeleine Delacorte was flirting with someone?" he said in surprise. "I guess it's never too late to come out of your shell. Who's the guy, or should I say gentleman?"

I described Milton Carruthers. "She seemed so enthralled with his attention, but I'm a little concerned about his intentions. He seemed to know all about the Delacorte family and their importance in Cadbury. He even seemed to know which Victorian house she lived in. He's a mystery writer and he mentioned doing research and I suppose he could have checked out Cadbury and read something about the Delacortes by chance. Or," I said with a sigh, "he made a move on her because of who she is."

"That's a tight spot to be in," he said.

"It sure is. I want to protect her, but she might not be happy with me interfering." I was still in Dane's arms and Julius had gotten impatient and was thwacking his tail as he threaded between both of our ankles. I looked into Dane's face. "You did a good job of straying from the subject, but it's not going to work anymore. Why don't you just tell me what you know."

"Even if I wanted to, there isn't anything to share," he said, torn between pulling me closer and dealing with the cat, who had grabbed on to his pant leg. "Lieutenant Borgnine made sure I was cut out of all the intel." He laughed. "He knows all about my weakness for your fabulous flirting ways."

"Really? You don't know anything?" I said.

He pulled away and went to the refrigerator. "I shouldn't tell you, but I think that Lieutenant Borgnine found out something about the victim to believe it wasn't a weird accident."

I came up behind him and hugged from the back as he opened the refrigerator. "In other words, murder. I knew you knew something."

"You better not let on you heard anything from me," he said. He brought up having to work bad shifts and on holidays. "It would also help if you didn't keep showing him up by solving cases." I promised I wouldn't tell, but not that I wouldn't keep investigating, and then I backed away as he took out the multi-wrapped stink fish.

"I hope you realize this is true love," he said, looking back at me as he held the can out at a distance.

I let Dane do the honors with the cat food before I started with the lemon bars. He grabbed his plate and headed to the back door. Julius, seeing that he had a new source for snacks, followed Dane and jumped on the counter to give his arm a rub before he went out the door. The cat even added a meow.

He'd offered to stay and be my sous chef but I made him leave. I was in a hurry and there was too much chance we'd get distracted.

Chapter 20

I put the large square tin filled with the lemon bars layered between sheets of waxed paper on top of the carrier with the sour cream biscuits that I'd already set into the bin on wheels and then added the small pink tin I'd filled with the sweets for Cloris. With all the extra help she'd given me, I was only too happy to bring her some treats. I still regretted how little I knew about her outside of the hotel and conference center. When this retreat was done, no more excuses that our schedules made it hard. I was going to arrange that girls' night I'd talked to Crystal about.

The Lodge was busy when I pulled the bin in and went to drop off Cloris's tin. I only got a moment with her since there was a lot of activity. People were checking the events of the evening and others had glasses of wine from the café and were sitting around the fireplace. People were coming in from outings like wine tours or whale watching, or enjoying the scenery along the 17-Mile Drive.

"Thank you," she said after I handed her the tin. She started to edge away, ready to deal with the guests, but I stopped her.

"After I left here, it occurred to me that the woman we saw start to come in but then leave could be the woman that man was looking for. You said her name was Brook Tanner," I said, prompting her to remember who I was talking about.

She had her eye on a couple that were headed our way as she answered my comment. "I suppose it could be, but the photo he showed me didn't really look like her."

"Have you seen Brook in anything but the loose clothes hidden under a baseball cap? I've seen her a couple of times and I couldn't even tell you what color her hair is or even how long it is."

"It doesn't really matter because he's gone," Cloris said, shrugging it off as the couple reached the counter. She thanked me again for the lemon bars and excused herself to take care of the guests.

Cloris was probably right that it didn't matter if Brook was the one that guy was looking for. She wasn't interested in passing along any information to Lieutenant Borgnine and neither was I. I had other things to deal with anyway, like the upcoming tea. I dragged the bin across the grounds to the Gulls building. Lucinda was already in the parlor setting up things for the tea. She turned and did a curtsey to show off the black uniform and white peaked hat.

"Sorry it's not Eileen Fisher," I joked.

"Tag saw the uniform and thinks I should wear it all the time, or at the very least some sort of standard wear." She shook her head, weary of all that went with dealing with him. "He's not good with random things or a lot of change. He's decided to create his own uniform of gray slacks with a white shirt and a black vest." She looked in the wheeled bin. "We might as well focus on the matter at hand. What did you bring?"

I showed her the lemon bars and the sour cream biscuits. She sampled both and gave them a nod of approval. The table we'd used before had a fresh tablecloth, and she had set out the three-tiered stands with plates and doilies on them. "The chef outdid himself," she said, opening the cooler and showing off the sandwiches he'd made. The egg salad was finely chopped with slivers of scallions. He'd created a salmon spread flavored with dill. I tasted one of the watercress on buttered brioche bread finger sandwiches and it was delicious. Somehow the butter worked perfectly with the leafy stems and tamed the pepper flavor. For our vegan, he'd made a spread with seasoned avocado. It hardly seemed English but would definitely please Rose Wilburn.

"I suppose I should thank him when I come to bake tonight," I said, and she chuckled.

"To keep the peace, you better not. I gave him a lot of praise and I didn't exactly tell him who was putting on the tea."

"You know that he's ridiculous. I go out of my way not to mess up what he considers his domain. And the way he takes his knives with him—as if I would even touch them."

"Chefs have a thing about their knives. He won't let Tag even look at them."

The ease of her manner and the subject of our conversation made it obvious she had no idea there'd been a death. I broke the news to her, but also reassured her that it was not one of my people. "Unfortunately, it's made them lose interest in solving Sammy's death and they want to play detective on the real case."

"Then I shouldn't expect random people coming up and asking me questions?" she said.

"There might be someone who hasn't given up, so you could get asked about where you were when the magician met his maker and want to see the bottom of your shoe to see if it matches the footprint that was one of the clues."

We were setting up as we talked. She wanted to know who the real corpse was and the details.

"I don't know anything about him, but I'm working on finding out what I can. Lieutenant Borgnine is going out of his way to keep me out of the loop. To the point that he's not even letting Dane in on details because he's afraid he'd tell me." I arranged two stacks of small plates, along with silverware and napkins. "And now that the group wants to play detective on a real case, I have to keep them from interfering and upsetting the lieutenant. I can't have him threatening to arrest any of them for getting in the middle of his investigation."

"They might like the experience since they're such crime enthusiasts," Lucinda said with a smile. She placed the plates of biscuits I'd made on one level of a three-tiered stand. She added pots of jam and clotted cream. "It might make them feel like they're part of the action." She paused a moment. "He certainly wouldn't arrest Madeleine."

"I don't think so since she is such a 'friend' to the police department. But who knows."

"If I can be of any help, let me know," she said. She stepped back from the table to check it over and gave me a thumbs-up. I went to open the glass door that closed the parlor off from the lobby of the Gulls building. Leslie and Victor Ackroyd got up from the seats they'd taken while they waited. When he got up, he started to take a step, but his wife stopped him and handed him the walking stick he'd left on the floor.

"I know you are tired of using this, but you still need it."

He looked around the area and seemed to be considering what she said. His gaze rested on the small group of the red-shirted business retreaters who had just come into the lobby and he grasped the stylish support pole. "You're right," he said. "I've come so far, there's no reason to blow it now."

There was a steady flow as the rest of my people arrived. I invited them to help themselves to the food while I kept a lookout for Madeleine to see who she was with. When there was no sign of her, I went out into the lobby to check. She and Milton Carruthers were slowly advancing through the living room–like setting. They were both wearing straw hats and appeared deep in conversation.

"Casey, I'm so sorry we're late. Milton and I were sitting outside and he read me the first chapter of his book. He knows all about investigating and such. We're going to work as a team to follow the clues."

"I said I'd be her Watson," the bearded author said, referring to Sherlock Holmes's sidekick.

"I thought I should be the 'Watson,'" Madeleine said. "Since I'm sure he has much more experience at solving crimes than I do, but he insisted that he'd take the secondary part."

I looked at Milton, or what I could see of him under the brim of the straw hat, and his gaze was locked on Madeleine. It was either sweet or sinister.

"We got them at the gift shop. It was Milton's idea," Madeleine said as she looked through the glass door at the group around the table. The only hat in the room was Bruce Elliott's, and the dark blue knit hat seemed more about keeping his shaved head warm than style.

I walked the couple in and showed off the table.

"You brought the clotted cream," Madeleine said in a pleased voice. She turned to Milton, and before she could explain, he nodded with understanding.

"How delightful. That makes this a cream tea, though a rather elaborate one."

Sandra Elliott overheard him and seemed puzzled. "Does that mean we have to put cream in our tea?" She made a face at the thought.

"It's not about what you put in your tea. It's about that." Milton Carruthers pointed out the bowl filled with what looked like soft yellow cream cheese. "It's for the biscuits, though to be authentic, I believe there should be scones." He urged her to try some and assured her it was like unsalted butter. He began describing all of the different sorts of meals that were called teas and their origin. Madeleine listened with rapt attention as he explained that in the old days in England there was a long span between their midday meal and dinner, which was served at eight or nine. In 1840, Anna, the seventh duchess of Bedford, found she was peckish around four in the afternoon and started requesting a tray with tea, bread and butter, and cake. It became a habit, and then she began inviting others to join her. He was just to the part about how women started dressing up for it when Bruce Elliott interrupted.

"That's interesting and all, but we need to get it together to figure out what happened to the guy this morning. We have to get going on it since it's already Friday night. Now that we've all given our statements to the cops, we're free to talk to each other about it. Right?" he said, looking at me.

"I suppose you can, but you could also put your heads together about what happened to the magician. Everything is still in place around the chalk outline," I said in a last-ditch effort to divert their attention. It failed with a thud.

"If given the choice of solving a fictious crime that has been set up for our amusement or using our mental energy to do something with actual value like capturing a real killer, I say we use our skills to go after the real one," Sandra Elliott said, sticking with her husband.

"But you're assuming it's murder," Leslie Ackroyd said. "I believe the police lieutenant was very specific that the cause of death hadn't been determined."

Bruce seemed impatient with her. "If we wait for that the weekend will be over. I say we assume it was homicide or murder and investigate it as such. While you people were knitting, I was looking around. As soon as our building was open again, I slipped up to the second floor. I couldn't look in the actual room, but I found a closet that had an orange extension cord like the one that was in the room. I'm sure it wasn't the actual one. The cops probably took it as evidence and they're checking it for fingerprints."

"So, what's your point?" Jenn Van Ness said. "We're not really going to get in the middle of a police investigation. This was supposed to be a fun, relaxing weekend while we untangled a puzzle." By now I was beginning to be able to keep track of what everybody's story was. Hers was that she was recently widowed and her daughter had brought her as a kind of treat, which seemed to be falling flat. She seemed kind of tense and I wondered if I should step in.

"Speak for yourself," Bruce said. "If there's a choice between a set-up game and a real live puzzle, I want the real one." Leslie and Victor Ackroyd let out hearty agreement.

"A real crime is a lot more interesting than a set-up one," Rose Wilburn said. "It'll certainly make a better story to tell when we go back to our regular lives."

Mary Smith seemed to be acting more as an observer. The rest of them didn't know that she'd brought Gary Moser into the tea reception the day before, but she knew that I knew that she had. She was in kind of a box. I doubted that she wanted to admit that she had any connection to him to the others for fear that they might peg her as a suspect. But if she didn't mention she'd brought him in, she might be worried that I would bring it up and then it would look like she was trying to hide something. I wasn't sure that she wasn't really hiding something. She must have decided that the safest thing to do was to say nothing.

"I think what my husband is trying to say is that's where the cord came from and anybody could have grabbed it, even though it was meant for the housekeepers," Sandra Elliott said.

Bruce surveyed the group. "I guess it's up to each of you if you want to be in or out of the investigation. But someone who is should talk to the housekeeper who found the victim. Get her story since she was there before any of us."

I tried to get their attention away from him before he suggested anything else. If Borgnine got wind that they were questioning people about Gary Moser's death, he'd have a fit. I had to protect them from themselves.

"Aside from the fact that I'm sure that housekeeper has gone for the day, you can't just start interrogating employees. It was different with the set-up death. All the designated suspects were told that any of you might question them. They were instructed to answer your questions, but if you were talking to real suspects about a real murder, believe me, they wouldn't be so anxious to talk to you and might not tell the truth."

"I bet I could tell," Victor Ackroyd said. "There was a whole podcast about how suspects have tells that show they're lying. Like looking anywhere but at the person asking the questions."

Emily Van Ness spoke to the group. "I've heard that too, like you can tell someone is lying if they won't look you in the eye. I think the secret is that we try to make it like conversation instead of an interrogation. Catch them off guard."

"Or we could stick to the original plan and use this opportunity to question her," Jenn Van Ness said, pointing to Lucinda.

Lucinda took a step toward them as if offering herself up, but this time Milton interceded. "Perhaps we should leave it up to Mrs. Maple, since she is the lead detective." He held his arm out as if to introduce

Madeleine. She was beaming and enjoying her moment.

"Thank you, Milton," she began. "This is turning out to be more exciting than I imagined. How can we possibly ignore what has happened in our midst? I agree that we should use our skills to do something useful." She looked around at everybody. "From what you've all said, you know a lot about solving mysteries from listening to podcasts, whatever they are, or in Milton's case, writing about them. I should think the police would be glad to have our help."

I was trying not to roll my eyes at what she'd said. Madeleine had this innocent nature and I was sure she believed they could offer Lieutenant Borgnine help—as in the more investigators, the merrier. But it was probably a lot closer to the adage that too many cooks spoiled the broth. She had no sense that the lieutenant would view it as interference.

Right now, I viewed my job as keeping them from doing anything that night. I couldn't stay and keep an eye on them and make sure they stayed out of trouble.

"As someone said, it's Friday evening. Why don't you take the night off from investigating and enjoy the activities provided by Vista Del Mar. If you have any room left after this lovely tea, I'm sure you'll enjoy a wonderful meal in the dining hall. After dinner, there are games available in the Lodge and a movie in Hummingbird Hall. There's always a popcorn wagon making loads of the fresh stuff. I heard they're showing *Knives Out*. Maybe it will inspire you." I felt the need to add something more. "And I may have some interesting information tomorrow."

"Does that mean you're investigating without us?" Bruce Elliott said.

"No, I'm just checking with a source. Tomorrow morning I'll share whatever I find out and we'll see where it leads us." I felt obligated to mention again that they shouldn't do anything that would upset the police.

"Maybe I should speak to Theodore," Madeleine said. I was the only one who understood she meant Lieutenant Borgnine. "I think he's still on the grounds."

"Don't," I said, almost in a squeal. "Everybody, just wait until the morning."

Chapter 21

"You have your work cut out for you," Lucinda said and I nodded. I'd already heard some of the group talk about taking a walk to the beach before they got ready for dinner and the evening activities. Bruce Elliott seemed to be the one who had gotten everybody riled up and I hoped he'd skip the walk since I wouldn't be there to calm them all down.

"When are you supposed to talk to your secret source?" Lucinda asked as she put the leftovers in a container and offered them to me. I took them thinking they would come in handy for dinner.

"We set up a time when I was sure I could be home," I said, reminding her that Vista Del Mar was unplugged and my cell phone had no reception. "It's my ex-boss Frank," I said. "I've never asked him before, but he has access to all kinds of databases and I thought he could give me some information I could throw to the wolves. I have to keep them from going off on their own and start poking around." I put my face in my hands. "You know I'll get the blame if they mess up the investigation. But with Madeleine so gung ho, I can't keep them out of it completely. I'm hoping I can keep them talking about possibilities, rather than following up on anything. If I have to, I'll do the actual investigating and let them watch or something."

"I get it. You'll be the sacrificial lamb and take the heat if anybody gets in trouble," Lucinda said and I nodded.

"I'm already in an awkward position. You probably didn't notice, but Gary Moser was at our tea reception yesterday. The group thinks he just came in looking for something, but it seemed to me that he was with Mary Smith—the woman with the white hair."

"I know who you mean. If mine would look like that, I'd gladly let it go natural." Lucinda's hair was an ash blond at the moment and was quite flattering, but Mary's hair was stunning. Lucinda started moving faster to load up the cart. "I have to get back before the dinner crowd starts. I asked one of the servers to help Tag if people show up before

I'm back, but I know he'll be thrown off if I'm not there. Tell me quickly about Mary Smith and the dead guy."

"She said he asked her to bring him in because he'd left something in the room, but I had the distinct impression that it was more than that. I'd already seen the guy hitting on a woman and then he seemed to be looking over my group as they came in."

"Was she looking around as she told you that?" Lucinda said with a chuckle. "If she did, it was a sign she was lying according to what one of them said."

"I didn't really notice. And that whole business of tells is kind of bogus." I grabbed one of the cucumber sandwiches out of the container she'd packed for me. I ate it in a couple of bites. The combination of the cucumbers with the cream cheese and the chef's special touch of adding some Everything But the Bagel seasoning was delicious. The tiny sandwich was just a tease and my appetite came alive and I started popping more of the leftover sandwiches.

"The group thinks that he came into the afternoon tea on his own. None of them know that he got a strong rebuke from a woman he made a move on the night before any of them arrived. Her name is Brook Tanner and she's got a whole other story. An unpleasant man showed up looking for someone and I think it might be her." I shook my head. "I've gotten way off the subject of Mary Smith. I don't know what's up with her."

"I get it. You don't want to say anything to sic the group on her as a suspect." She was moving faster and was almost finished clearing everything off.

"It could be something or not, just like Brook Tanner and that man." I grabbed one of the biscuits that I'd made and slathered it with the last of the clotted cream and took a bite. "Too delicious, if I say so myself." I finished it off and looked at my watch. "Maybe Frank will have some amazing information."

"Like I said, you have your hands full with this group." Lucinda pulled off the tablecloth and stuck it on the cart and did a count of the cups and plates. "I'll be all ears when you come to the Blue Door to bake tonight. But for now, I have to get there before Tag has a panic attack. He was beside himself last night because when I brought everything back there was a cup missing. That is just the kind of thing that pushes him over the edge." She looked around at the couches and chairs in the inviting room. "I suppose it rolled under something." She let out a mirthless laugh. "I finally told him it had gotten broken and that seemed to end it. Do me a favor and make the cup disappear if it turns up. It would start a whole other problem if he found out I made it up to calm him down." She shook her head. "What happened to that fun guy I knew in high school," she said wistfully. I held the door for her and she wheeled the cart out of the room and sped away.

And she thought I had my hands full. This group was just here for the weekend. Tag was a permanent fixture. I considered moving the furniture to check for the missing cup, but I was running out of time. I did a last check on the room to make sure that nobody had left something in there and then I left. I was deep in thought, trying to come up with a way I could let the group have their way at playing detective but keep them out of trouble. As I opened the glass door outward, I heard an *umph* sort of sound. I looked up to see the source and a red shirt came into focus, then the neck and head attached to it, and I realized I'd hit him with the door.

"Sorry," I said to a proper-looking man. His red shirt was carefully tucked in a pair of khaki pants. My instant impression was of someone who spent a lot of time inside. I realized it was his coloring, which could be described as pale or pasty-faced. His hair was neatly parted on the side and was a medium shade of brown. Other than the shirt that made him stand out, he would have been great doing surveillance.

He accepted my apology gracefully and seemed more interested at looking into the room that I was leaving. "Is the afternoon tea over? Is there going to be another one tomorrow? Is it open to everyone?" He didn't wait for me to answer, but went on about how much he enjoyed a proper afternoon tea and explained that he had worked for the company's UK office for a couple of years. "I like the way your group is dressed," he said, looking down at his shirt. "These are stupid, but someone said it was necessary to make us seem like a tribe." He didn't seem impressed with the idea. He looked down at the container full of leftovers in my hand. It was far more than I could eat and I invited him to help himself.

"Lemon bars aren't exactly traditional, but they're my favorite," he said, taking one. He had more questions about our group and I explained what I did with retreats. "They are usually just about yarn craft, but this one has a mystery component." Now that I'd told him about my group, I was curious about his.

"We are far less interesting than a group of people dressing up like they're from some other time, sipping tea and checking out clues. We're much less fun, too," he added. "We're claims adjusters." He let it sit a moment then went into detail about what claims adjusters did. He cut right to it and said their job was to negotiate a settlement on a claim.

"You mean figure out how to pay as little as possible?" I said and he reluctantly agreed.

"People try to pull scams all the time. Pretending to be more injured than they are. We're here to brainstorm ways of not overpaying on claims." He handed me his card and I saw his name was Sander Petrillo and his office was in San Jose. He seemed so unconcerned; I wondered if he knew that someone had died.

I skirted the issue, asking him if he'd noticed any excitement earlier in the day. "We left right after breakfast for a spear fishing trip. It was supposed to sharpen our killer instincts," he said. "Did we miss something?"

The image of a bunch of people in red shirts shooting fish and leaving blood in the water seemed pretty disgusting, but I tried to appear benign. Kevin St. John had become very good at being discreet about bad things that happened at Vista Del Mar, and the majority of the guests probably never knew. The ambulance was the only vehicle that made a stir and it was gone quickly. All the activity was confined to the Sand and Sea building. The rest of the buildings that housed guest rooms were spread over the hundred-plus acres of sloping terrain, so even if they'd been on the grounds they might have missed it.

Lieutenant Borgnine only focused on the few people who were close to the crime scene, and since he wore the rumpled jacket wasn't recognized as the police by most of the guests. In other words, there was nothing to stir up people's curiosity, and the manager made a point not to have the staff talking about anything that happened.

I might have just let it go but Sander had asked me a direct question. It was my nature that when I was asked a straightforward question, I gave an honest answer. If my mother had ever asked me how I really felt about my life instead of putting me on the defensive by giving her spiel of being a wife, mother and doctor when she was my age, I would have told her the truth. I wasn't happy with the way I had trouble sticking with careers and places. It worried me that the more I seemed to have ties to Cadbury, the more likely it was that I would feel trapped and do something like suddenly take up the offer of cooking school in Paris or the detective academy in Los Angeles.

My mind had wandered off and I realized that Sander was waiting for an answer.

"There was a death this morning," I said. Even though I hadn't heard it officially stated, it was pretty obvious what had happened. "A man was electrocuted while using a hair dryer." I didn't say if it was homicide or an accident or identify him and was going to let it go, but then Sander said something surprising, but when I thought about it, not unexpected.

"I'm sure glad our company doesn't handle the insurance for this place."

• • •

Everybody sees things through their own perspective, I thought as I rushed home. It had been a whole negotiation about when Frank would

142

call and I didn't want to miss it. The kitchen was dim when I walked in and I almost didn't see Julius as he came in to greet me. He jumped on the counter to check out the container of sandwiches I had set down.

"I know, they don't smell strong enough to please you." I used *strong* instead of *bad*, trying not to be judgmental. He looked up at me with a reproachful nod anyway. "So many questions," I said to the feline. "How did you make it from kittenhood to a grown-up cat? Did you ever have a home? How did you end up on the Vista Del Mar grounds taunting Kevin St. John?" That was where I'd first seen the black cat as Kevin St. John barely missed running over him with a golf cart. As far as I was concerned that was one more reason to not like the manager. Julius didn't even give me a meow, just looked at me with an arresting stare. "I guess it'll always be your secret." I gave his back a stroke. "You picked the right house to show up at. Who else would deal with this." I was already taking out the can of stink fish.

Frank's call was due any minute and I rushed to go through the whole unwrapping of the can with my cell phone nearby. I'd hoped to finish with the stinky stuff before I had to deal with the phone. But of course, it didn't happen. I answered and hit the speaker button just as I was about to drop the dab of fish in Julius's dish. Between holding my nose to avoid the stench and the way bending over affected my voice, I knew I would sound strange. I told Frank what was going on and he agreed to let me finish before we talked.

I had dealt with the rewrapping and washed my hands twice with lemon soap to rid any remnant of pink stink and was sitting at the kitchen table when the phone rang again.

"Cat fed?" Frank asked. After I'd uttered a yes, he went on about how I should really try the cat food he fed Mittens. It smelled delicious, like prime rib. I was still getting used to the idea that the gruff PI had a cat with a name like that. In a moment of softness, Frank told me that he'd found the kitten on a cold night while he was doing a surveillance.

The container of sandwiches was right in front of me and all the talk of prime rib and delicious smells had reawakened my hunger and I grabbed one of the sandwiches, hoping to get it swallowed before he noticed. "I'm sure you're in a hurry," I said. "Let's get to the point." There was still a residue of sandwich in my mouth and I had to chew and swallow.

It was usually Frank I caught eating a submarine sandwich or a donut, but this time it was me. He joked about his investigative skills when it came to someone eating. He wanted details.

"Finger sandwiches," he said with a laugh after I'd told him about the afternoon tea. "Any scones and clotted cream?"

"No scones, but there were biscuits that I made and we had clotted cream." I noticed that Lucinda had included one of the biscuits spread with the thick butter-like mixture and my mouth was watering imagining the taste. Finally, I couldn't resist and took a bite.

"When you send those cookies, maybe you can put in some biscuits." I laughed and quickly swallowed and let out a satisfied sigh.

"So tell me what you know," I said.

"As expected, there were a number of Gary Mosers. If you have any more details, we might be able to pick the right one.

"I know the guy here was from Santa Clara. I'm guessing he was early fifties," I said.

"Could be this guy. I'll send you his picture." There was a ding on my phone and a photo showed up. "Is this him?" Frank asked.

"Yes. It looks like a mug shot," I said, looking at the photo of only his head. His expression seemed flat or maybe grim. "Was he arrested for something?" I heard Frank laugh and then the squeak of him shifting in his recliner desk chair.

"No. Guess again, Feldstein."

"Really, are you going to make this into a game?"

"Yes," he said with a chortle. "Let's see you use your skills—which you can thank me for."

"Frank, I only worked for you for two weeks and it was all phone work."

"But just being around me, you must have heard and seen a lot," he said.

"So, I got it by osmosis?"

"Yes, I like that," he said. "Now, look at the picture again and think about where it came from." I stared at the image on the screen of my phone. Then the obvious struck me. "It's from an identification badge.

"Very good. I'd let you figure out what kind but it's Friday night here and I've got places to be, so I'll cut to the chase. This Gary Moser is a licensed PI and ta-da," he said with a flourish, "a former cop."

I wanted to talk about him more, but since Frank had made time an issue, I wanted to give him Brook Tanner's name to see what came up. I could hear the click of the keyboard as I reminded him about the encounter I'd seen between her and Gary.

He shot me another photo. "Is this her?" It was hard to tell because it was from a distance with other people. The woman was wearing an evening gown and had a blown-out hairstyle.

"It could be," I said and explained the problem. "What can you tell me? Who is she?"

"It's not so much who she is as much as who she's married to. Her profession is listed as an earring designer," he said with a chuckle. "But she's married to Reynolds Tanner. He's a venture capitalist who made a huge fortune from getting money for startups that actually made a profit."

Without my asking, Frank sent a picture of Reynolds and it was the man I'd seen. Frank mumbled as he read something. "This is from a newspaper article about how some charity event brought together Reynolds's wives. Brook seems to be the latest one." I heard him let out a *hmm*. "He seems to have a pattern, judging from the dates for each of his marriages mentioned in the article. He has a turnover rate of about seven years per wife. Except her, he's into the eighth year with her." Frank let out a lascivious chortle. "She must have special talents."

I heard a woman's voice in the background and then what sounded like a smooch on his cheek after he greeted her. "Are you sending me a picture?" I said in a teasing tone.

"You wish," he said. "Got to go." And then there was silence. He had really come through this time with aces, but now I had to figure what to do with what I knew.

Chapter 22

I had to sit a minute after hanging up with Frank. Gary Moser was a PI and a former cop? That didn't mean that he wasn't on the prowl for companionship, but he could have been on a job. I was definitely going to send Frank a big box of cookies. I never would have gotten that information on my own. Ditto about Brook Tanner. Julius jumped in my lap and surprised me by making it clear it was just about affection. He butted his head against my chin and actually gave me a tiny kitty kiss with his sandpaper tongue. The only downside was it smelled of stink fish.

Julius wasn't one for prolonged cuddling and jumped off my lap. I took some time to check for phone messages, emails and texts. There was a message from my father asking me to please call my mother because she was frantic and on the verge of calling Sammy to make sure I was okay. I didn't want her calling him. He'd tell her about this weekend and how he was being a corpse for me. I just didn't have it in me to deal with a phone call with her just then. Maybe if it had been a friendly girlfriend call just sharing news, I would have felt differently. But I always felt on the defensive and she was judgmental. The only answer was to send her a text explaining I was in the midst of a retreat and that I would call her when I had a moment. She hated getting texts from me, but at least it would count as a response and keep her from getting Sammy in the middle of it. I wondered how she'd feel if I told her that Sammy had his eye on someone else.

I had planned to let the group be on their own for dinner and the evening activities, but I was worried some of them might ignore what I'd said and play detective. Now that I knew Gary Moser was a PI and former cop, it seemed even more important they not interfere. For my own peace of mind, I wanted to try to distract them.

I did a spruce up of my appearance and grabbed something I thought might help get their minds on something else. By now it was dark and the lights on the stone posts illuminated the entrance to the driveway. There was a flow of people in the area between the dining hall and the Lodge as people finished dinner and went to the social hall to hang out.

My group was still in the dining room spread between two of the big round tables. The food service was at the end, but I managed to get a plate with some lasagna and salad. I knew the sauce would pale in comparison to Dane's, but it was hot and I was hungry even with the snacks Lucinda had given me. As I viewed the groups at the two tables, I decided who I was most worried about going off on their own. Bruce Elliott seemed a likely candidate, and there was Madeleine and Milton Carruthers. I was worried about more than them pretending to be Nick and Nora Charles. Was he just after companionship, maybe a weekend fling, or was he looking to get entrenched in their family? Cora wouldn't approve no matter what his intentions were.

"I thought we were on our own," Madeleine said when I pulled out a chair at her table. Bruce Elliott and his wife were across the table. She was eating her dessert, appearing to be lost in her own thoughts, and he was checking out the room with a hawk-like gaze.

"I had some time and I always like to keep an eye on things," I said, looking at Bruce and then back at the couple.

I tried not to stare, but Madeleine and Milton were sitting very close together and I almost said something. I chided myself, realizing I was becoming like my mother. Madeleine was an adult and could do what she wanted. But I also felt responsible for her. For a moment, I considered pulling him aside and asking him about his plans. Just as I was thinking how inappropriate that would be, Cora Delacorte marched into the dining hall. She was done up in a gold dress with a jacket and had put on extra green eye shadow. She seemed perturbed as she came toward the table. She eyed Milton Carruthers and how his arm was almost touching Madeleine's.

"Who are you?" she demanded. I felt obligated to step in and handle the introductions. Milton was very gentlemanly. He stood and took Cora's hand. "I was just telling Mrs. Maple that I hoped I'd get to meet her sister and here you are."

Cora softened for a moment and then shook her head in annoyance at her sister's new identity. "Madeleine, did you forget the historical society event."

"I thought I'd skip it," Madeleine said.

"Skip it? You can't skip it. We're benefactors. I brought a dress for you. You can change in the ladies' room."

Madeleine turned to Milton. "Would you like to join us?" He was in the process of nodding a yes when Cora cut him off.

"Everything is arranged. You can't simply decide to bring someone along at the last minute." She looked at him directly. "And it's black tie. I'm sure you didn't pack a tuxedo."

She let Cora hustle her off and barely got a chance to touch his arm and say goodbye. At least now I didn't have to worry about Madeleine getting into trouble with Milton.

"Is the woman with the green eyeshadow part of the mystery?" Rose Wilburn asked from the other table. "The way she keeps showing up and dragging Mrs. Maple away."

"No, they're just sisters." I didn't want to give away too much about their relationship or their position in the town and just said that they were at different points in their lives. I waited for everything to settle and finally got to why I'd come. Rather than trying to get them not to think about something, I'd decided it was better to give them something else to concentrate on.

"We've gotten so caught up in the mystery part of the weekend that the knitting has been kind of kicked to the corner." I took out a pair of completed hand warmers and handed them to Sandra Elliott to pass them around to the group and urged them to try them on.

Bruce Elliott started to hand them off with no regard, but as an afterthought put them on. He inspected his hands with a critical eye. Then he held up his hands and wiggled his fingers. "I thought these were going to be too girly, but as long as it's this brown yarn, they're okay." He looked at his hands again. "They feel good, too." He took out his phone and tried typing. "It works if you want to do texts and social media posts," he said.

Rose Wilburn had gotten up and was standing behind Bruce. Her gaze was stuck on the phone and she mumbled "social media post" in a wistful voice. She straightened and pulled herself together. "How silly of me. I thought he really had Facebook on his phone."

"I wanted to give you a pep talk on the project and I thought if you actually tried them on, you'd have a different feeling about working on them. They'll be a souvenir of your weekend here and something that you will really use. They're easy to knit and the only issue is that unless you're a super knitter like Sandra Elliott, you'll have to pay attention to the changes from knits to purls," I said. "When you have some free time, you can use our meeting room or you could gather in the lobby of your building," I said, not adding what I was thinking—that paying attention to their knitting would keep them from talking about Gary Moser's demise.

"I like that line about them being a remembrance of the weekend," Mary Smith said, jotting it down.

Jenn Van Ness seemed to be in a disagreement with her daughter, but set it aside as she looked over the knitted pieces when they came to her. Victor and Leslie Ackroyd looked up from their conversation when the hand warmers reached them. They tried them on as well, commenting on starting a trend. Milton Carruthers seemed interested in the hand warmers for his park ranger sleuth and then looked at the empty chair next to him. "I'd hoped to spend some time knitting with Madeleine," he said, sounding disappointed. Seeing and trying on the finished product had actually made a difference and they all showed some interest in working on them outside of the workshops.

I hoped that between the movie and whatever time they spent knitting, they wouldn't have a chance to get in trouble. I thought my job was done and I'd even managed to pick at the lasagna at the same time. I got up to leave, thinking I'd taken care of everything.

"Hey, weren't you supposed to be getting some inside information?"

Bruce Elliott said. I should have known that he'd remember what I'd said. Now I regretted saying anything. I stalled him and said we'd talk it over in the morning. Emphasis on the *talk it over* part.

No surprise, he didn't take it well and started complaining that they should have free rein to investigate and not be in my control. I couldn't think of a good answer, so I simply said I had to go.

I went through the Lodge on my way out. The social hall was abuzz with activity and there was a din of voices and the thwack of the table tennis paddles hitting the small balls. Cloris was behind the counter leaning on her elbow.

"Do you ever go home?" I said with a laugh. Her clothes looked crisp, but she was beginning to look frazzled.

"Once in a while," she joked. "But the night clerk called in sick, so I'm here for the night. I'm trying to conserve my energy."

"I hate to give you anything else to deal with," I began. "I'm doing my best to keep my group out of the actual investigation of what happened to Gary Moser. But I'm a little concerned by one guy in the group." I described him as having a shaved head and complaining a lot.

"I know exactly who you mean. Room 109, right?" I nodded and said his name was Bruce Elliott. She launched into his numerous complaints. "It went from the sheets being like sandpaper to Sammy's acting not being up to snuff. He definitely has a sense of entitlement and I could imagine him deciding to go rogue." Cloris shifted elbows. "His poor wife seemed relieved to let him complain to someone else. She threw me an apologetic look, but then she walked away and let him keep dumping on me." Cloris promised to keep her eyes peeled as much as she could, being stuck in the Lodge.

"It didn't help that I had said I was getting some new information that I would share and then I didn't." I explained why and Cloris agreed. Then she asked me what it was.

"It's about who Gary Moser was. He was a licensed PI and a former cop."

"Oh," she said, surprised. "How long ago was he a cop?" she asked.

All I could do was tell her the truth, which was that I didn't know. "My source was in a hurry. Hot date," I said, and she laughed again. "This is crazy," I said. "I think you know more about Frank than I know about you." I told her about my idea for the girls' night when I was done with my retreat.

"I'd love that," she said. "But there isn't much to know. Like you said, this place and my classes are my life right now."

"You didn't just hatch," I said. "You came from somewhere and have a family."

"I'll tell you everything you want to know when we have that girls' night. For now, I'm trying to conserve my mental energy to get through tonight."

"I know what you mean. I still have a night of baking ahead." I offered to get us each a red-eye from the café—coffee with a shot of espresso—and then we toasted to burning the candle at both ends. I promised to bring her some muffins when I brought the supply for the café.

Chapter 23

By the time I pulled my yellow Mini Cooper into one of angled parking spots in downtown Cadbury, all the stores and restaurants were shut down or close to it. Even on a Friday night, everything closed early. The only exception was the twenty-four-hour pharmacy. If anyone wanted late night food, they had to go to Sand City for a McDonald's.

As I lugged the grocery bags with ingredients for the muffins, I looked down Grand Street and saw the light from the pharmacy spreading on the sidewalk in front of it. I always found it comforting to know that there was something open even in the wee hours when I was baking at the Blue Door.

I was prepared to tell Lucinda about my call with Frank, but when I got inside, she had her hands full with Tag. I chuckled when I saw that he was wearing the gray slacks, white shirt and black vest she'd said he was going to make his uniform. He seemed agitated about something and Lucinda shook her head as she caught a look at the story on the back of the menu she'd dropped into the holder on the side of the host stand.

What the fairy-tale story about their relationship left out was how time had changed them. Not so much Lucinda. I'm sure she always loved nice clothes and makeup, though maybe her love of designer wear had come later. As for makeup—I couldn't remember ever seeing her without lipstick. The problem was Tag. I gathered he'd always had a precise kind of personality, but over time it had gotten too precise. His being hysterical about the number of cups returning to the restaurant compared to how many had left was typical.

She was trying to get him out of there and he was rechecking each place setting. He did smile when he saw me and asked about the missing cup. Not wanting to cause a problem, I went along with Lucinda's story that it had gotten broken. It wasn't a lie because if I found it, I intended to make that true.

The chef came out clutching his backpack with his beloved knives. He gave me the same look he always did, as if I was going to destroy the kitchen. He watched Tag fussing with the place settings and Lucinda trying to get him to stop doing it and edged his way out the door.

I got out of their way and went to the kitchen. A few minutes later, Lucinda called out they were leaving and then there was quiet. I did my usual of turning on soft jazz and looked out at the street as I went back through the main dining area. I half expected to see someone rolling up the sidewalk.

I was glad to have some peace for the moment as I began to think over all that had happened at Vista Del Mar. It seemed like days ago instead of just hours ago since I'd followed the scream with my retreat group. There was too much adrenaline flowing and I hadn't thought to look around the room. All I really remembered was the orange extension cord and Gary Moser wrapped in the green shower curtain.

We were rushed out of there before I'd had a chance to process what I'd seen.

I was on autopilot as I rolled out the crust for the apple pies. If it hadn't been for my retreat group deciding they could solve what happened to him, I would have stayed out of it. It would have been so simple if they'd stuck to the game we'd set up. I was still struggling with how I could deal with the group and keep them out of trouble.

The answer seemed to be to keep it like a game. I could share what I knew, but keep it to brainstorming sessions in the safety of the meeting room. I was going over random thoughts I could feed to the group. Like what about the housekeeper? Supposing she screamed after she'd killed him. I was sure nobody suspected her. He'd been there for a few days. Maybe he tried to have his way with her. I laughed at my choice of words. It sounded old-fashioned, like something that belonged in our original game.

Random thoughts seemed to come out of nowhere. It had to be someone who knew about the cord. What about the hair dryer?

Someone needed access to the room and to know when he was in the shower. These were all good prompts I could give the group. Anything to keep them talking.

The pies were in the oven when I heard the tap on the door. Even though I was pretty sure who it was, I looked out through the glass portion of the door to check.

"I'm glad to see that you take precautions," Dane said as I invited him in. He was in uniform, which made giving him a hug a challenge. "What are we baking tonight?"

Apple pies and chocolate cake for the Blue Door, banana nut muffins for the coffee places and a lot of biscuits for the Saturday event. It seems that the guests got wind of what we'd served for the afternoon teas and requested some of the same food.

"Sorry I can only offer you help during my break," he said, following me into the kitchen. "You can try using your comedy flirty skills to get me to give up what I know."

"Why should I waste my talents," I said. "You already told me that Borgnine is keeping you out of the loop."

He made a disappointed face. "I forgot I told you."

"And," I said, "I know something you don't know." I put the pies in the oven and got ready to start on the muffins.

"Really?" he said, surprised. Then he grinned. "Are you going to make me flirt with you to get you to give it up?"

I rolled my eyes. "I don't think you need a reason to flirt with me."

"You're right." He reached out and twirled a strand of my hair around his finger as he gave me a simmering look.

"It's not fair that you're so much better at it than I am." I shook my head in mock annoyance.

"I could give you lessons," he said, taking the strand of hair and putting it behind my ear.

"I'm beginning to think it's one of those things you either can do or you can't," I said. "It's probably best that I leave it as comedy relief." All this playing with my hair had made me realize I needed to get it out of the way and pulled it back with a scrunchy. He gave me a look of mock disappointment now that he had no strands of hair to play with.

The radio on his shoulder began to squawk, reminding him that he was only there for a short time. "So, what do I have to do to find out what you know?"

"How about you deal with stink fish for a week?" I said.

"Aren't you the romantic. Sure, if that's what it takes."

I told him about Gary Moser's current profession and his past one. Dane leaned against the counter and rocked his head. "That's definitely worth stink fish details." Then he wanted to know how I found out. "I know there have been some officers on the grounds. Did you try the flirting move on one of them?" he asked.

"I would never cheat on you and flirt with somebody else for information." I ran my finger on his bare arm and half closed my eyes. Surprisingly he didn't laugh.

"That was a really good move," he said, looking down where my fingers had trailed. "And I'm so relieved to know that you are saving all your flirty moves for me." He sounded like he was teasing, but I knew he meant it. "So, then where did you get it."

"Frank," I said. "It's only costing me a box of cookies." I explained that he had access to databases.

Dane got serious after that. "I wonder if Moser was on a job?"

I nodded. "And I think I know who he might have been working for."

The radio squawked again. Someone had gotten their arm stuck in a mailbox.

"Not him again," Dane said, shaking his head. "It's not the first time he's written a letter and then had second thoughts, always in the middle of the night." He looked around the kitchen and spied a can of shortening. "That'll work to get his arm to slide out. Leave a note and tell Lucinda Cadbury PD will replace it." He gave me a quick kiss before he went to the door.

The restaurant seemed quiet with him gone and I got lost in baking. I didn't even want to look at the clock when I finished. The pies were on their pedestals, the frosted chocolate cake under a glass doom and a carrier with the biscuits for the Saturday night event sat on the counter when I finally went to the door. I dropped off the containers of muffins at the coffee spots and when there was only the one for the café at Vista Del Mar and a special package for Cloris left in the car, I headed for home.

It felt like the world belonged to me as I drove home down the deserted streets. I pulled in my driveway and then for what seemed like the millionth time went across the street to make the delivery. The lights were off in most of the buildings, which made them disappear into the darkness. The rush of the ocean cut through the silence and I could smell it in the air now that all the fireplaces were cold. I heard a rustle in the undergrowth along the side of the road and a deer stumbled out, giving me a quizzical look.

The lights were on in the Lodge. It was the only building that was always illuminated and always open. Cloris was leaning on her arm and looked up when I walked in.

"Thank you," she said when I handed her the muffins I'd brought for her. She came out from behind the counter and opened the door to the café so I could leave the container of muffins. She did some stretches and yawned. "It's good to have a reason to move around."

I asked her if there'd been any problems with my group. She shook her head. "Lieutenant Borgnine was here again," she said with a sigh.

"What did he want?" I asked.

"He didn't talk to me. Just to Mr. St. John."

I left her to her vigil. The darkness was a shock after the lights inside and it took a while for my eyes to adjust. A car turned into the driveway with its headlights turned off. I watched as it pulled into the small parking lot nearby. I heard a car door opening. I was curious who had been out so late and positioned myself where I couldn't be seen as someone got out and started to walk away. I kept at a distance as I trailed them, though it was so dark, I doubted I would have been seen. It became obvious that the person was headed to the Gulls building. As they went up the stair to the small front porch, the outdoor light illuminated the figure and I recognized Brook Tanner.

Chapter 24

Cloris was behind the counter when I stopped by on the way to breakfast. "You're still here," I said, surprised that she appeared alert and looked put-together, too.

"Mr. St. John came in and I was able to catch a nap," she said. She assured me that the muffins I'd brought for the café had been found and were on display in a basket. And the ones I'd brought her had been enjoyed. She held up the empty container and pushed it across the wooden counter.

"After I left you, I saw something strange," I said. Cloris perked up and asked for details.

"Brook Tanner came back from somewhere," I said. "Any idea where she'd been?"

Cloris straightened. "I heard that she's done that before." She paused. "More than once." That was all Cloris would say but I was sure she had thoughts about where the woman had gone. Cloris seemed to be being extra cautious about saying anything even to me.

"Did you know that Gary Moser was a PI?" I asked, not remembering if I'd told her or not. "I wonder if she was the case he was working on and she figured it out. When she snapped at him, it wasn't to repel his romantic advances."

"I don't know. It's the discretion thing. As long as it's not illegal and there's no unwanted touching, I try to stay out of it," she said. "I don't want to give Mr. John any ammunition to take to the Delacortes. Even when Lieutenant Borgnine questioned me again, I just answered his specific questions and didn't respond when he asked me if any guests had done anything out of the ordinary." She seemed troubled. "I can't get in trouble for not saying something, can I?"

"I guess it depends on what you don't say," I said. I could see she felt caught in the middle between giving Kevin any grounds to get rid of her and being truthful to the cops. "My rule is that if anyone asks me a direct question, I answer it, but something vague like that—" I shrugged as an answer.

"I could tell you what I'm concerned about," she said. She had been so helpful to me so many times, I was glad to do something for her that might ease her mind.

"Don't worry, I won't tell Kevin," I said. She still blanched at me referring to him by his first name.

"It's about Brook Tanner," she began. "She wanted me to cash a big check for her. I couldn't because we didn't have the cash to cover it. That's what I didn't tell." She let out a heavy sigh.

"There was nothing illegal about that, or any unwanted touching involved, unless she pinched you when you said no." I smiled to lighten things up. "And you didn't even cash the check. So, what was there to tell anyway?"

"Thank you," Cloris said, smiling with relief. "That's what I thought. By the way, I remembered that she said she was here for a spiritual retreat."

I wondered what kind of spiritual retreat had her going out somewhere late at night and needing a hunk of cash.

I could smell the pancakes as soon as I left the Lodge and joined the people walking to the dining hall. Actually, I was more interested in the coffee and lots of it to clear my tired feeling. It was taking a lot of mental effort to figure out how I could use what I knew with my group. The good news, there would be nothing for them to investigate, since I had all the information already.

Just like people seemed to return to the same seats in the meeting room, once they'd chosen a table in the dining hall, they went back to it all weekend. This group was no different. Mary Smith was in the exact seat she'd been sitting in when I'd joined her at lunch the previous day. Bruce and Sandra Elliott were at the other table. Jenn Van Ness was carrying a tray toward the table where her daughter was already sitting with a cup of coffee. Rose Wilburn arrived with her food and did something odd. She took the plates off the tray and then stuck a fork in the food before pulling out a couple of the flowers from the vase on the lazy Susan and placing it next to her plate. She angled her phone and took a few pictures. When she looked up and realized I was watching her, she grew embarrassed and messed with the arrangement, quickly putting the flower back in the vase.

The Ackroyds arrived and Leslie told Victor to sit while she got the food. He stowed the walking stick under the table and reached for the vacuum pot on the lazy Susan and poured himself a cup of coffee. "I wish they had a more interesting blend than coffee that comes ground in a can." Bruce Elliott picked up that someone had offered a complaint and jumped in.

"You could say the same about the pancakes." Bruce shook his head with distaste. "Clearly a mix. And the fruit—a few grapes and hunks of melon. Where are the berries and soft pineapple?" His wife nudged him and he glared at her. "I have a right to my opinion."

When I looked up Madeleine was crossing the large room with Milton Carruthers just behind her carrying a tray loaded with plates. She had found yet another suit in a nubby beige color. Cora hadn't managed to keep her from coming back after the charity event. Milton seemed like a nice person. I didn't want to believe that the attention he was giving Madeleine had to do with her wealth and position. But it was a possibility. It was a little creepy the way he'd described their house as if he'd had it under surveillance.

What made it even more difficult was how much she seemed to be enjoying his attention. She'd never told me about the "boys" in her life. From what I knew it seemed like anywhere she'd gone she'd been heavily chaperoned. If she didn't have a lot or maybe any experience, she would have no judgment. I didn't want her to have a romantic disaster on my watch.

I waited until they were all situated, and after asking if anyone needed anything, I went to get my food. I glanced around at the crowd as I threaded through the tables. Brook Tanner was sitting at a table next to the window. A couple was sitting across the table involved in their own conversation. And two lone men were sitting several seats apart. She seemed enthralled in something she was reading. Her plate was pushed away, still loaded with half-eaten food. She seemed to have no contact with anyone else at the table, but it could have been just for show. I eliminated the man in the floppy hat and ancient polo shirt. But the other guy showed more promise. He was around her age and had his sunglasses tucked in his shirt and wore one of those watches that did a lot of things and was waterproof. I imagined them going off kayaking on Monterey Bay. When I checked the table behind her, I recognized one of Dane's fellow officers dressed in jeans and a sweatshirt sitting with a plate of food. Was it just a complimentary breakfast or was he keeping an eye on her?

I came back to the table and began to work on the food. I didn't care what Bruce Elliott said about the pancakes, they tasted good to me. As did the scrambled eggs and hash browns. I did agree with him about the fruit, though. I wondered if he'd complained about the afternoon tea. I didn't want to hear it if he had.

I was reaching for the coffee pot to refill my coffee when Bruce caught my eye.

"You said you were going to share some inside information," he said. The way he'd said "inside information," I had the feeling he was going to find a way to dismiss it. But that was irrelevant at the moment because there was no way I was going to say anything about the case in the dining room, where eager ears could be nearby.

Kevin St. John was trying to keep Gary Moser's death and the investigation on the down low. I might view him as my adversary, but in this case, I could see his point. I felt certain the crowd at the tables nearby had no idea anything had happened. They were close enough that I could hear them talking about an excursion to Carmel. And they certainly would be able to hear us. They might gloss over a discussion of knitting, but if they heard words like *murder* and *dead guy*, they'd be tuning in.

"I'm saving that for during the knitting workshop. When it's just us," I said, giving a subtle gesture toward the other diners.

Bruce Elliott didn't seem happy that he hadn't gotten his way, but he eyed the nearby tables and seemed to understand.

After that the discussion turned to the movie from the night before. Bruce said he'd figured out the ending of *Knives Out,* and I hoped everybody at the nearby tables had seen the movie because he gave a play-by-play description of how he'd figured out the clues.

We all went our own ways for the free time after breakfast before the yarn workshop. I decided Victor was right about the coffee in the dining hall. I still felt groggy and stopped in the café for a red-eye. I was hanging by the counter when Emily Van Ness came in. I looked around, expecting to see her mother, but she was alone.

She noticed me as she placed her order for a black eye. "Two shots of expresso," I said. "That's hard-core."

"I need it. This weekend isn't working out the way I'd hoped," she said and made a weary face.

"I'm sorry," I said. My instant reaction was to take it personally and I suggested we get a table. "Maybe I can help."

I led the way to a spot in the corner that afforded some privacy. It was next to the window and I looked out at the view. A group in shorts with binoculars who I guessed were bird-watchers had crossed the area called the grass circle and were entering the boardwalk that led through the sand dunes to the beach. The white sky was almost the same color as the pale sand.

"Why don't you tell me about it." I took a long sip of the strong coffee drink, preparing for whatever she was going to say.

"I don't know what I thought would happen. Maybe that she'd be happy with what I did and me," she began. "But there's just no pleasing my mother."

"Don't I know about that," I said, then stopped myself from going any further. This was about her.

"I know she's been having a tough time since her husband died. You heard how upset she was at being a widow. I thought she'd be happy to come back to this area. It took a lot of planning to make it a surprise. She didn't know until we got on the plane that we were coming here. She's fascinated by all those true crime shows on TV, and she used to knit a lot." Emily drank off some of her coffee, giving me a chance to say something.

"You said your mother's husband. Then he wasn't your father?" She shook her head and said her parents had gotten divorced years earlier. "I wasn't really close with Jack. They got married when I was in high school, and you know how it is," she said with a shrug. "I was off with my friends most of the time. And then I went to college. I just listed us as Van Ness to make it less confusing. But her last name now is Peltier. It's funny how her initials now are the same as they were when she was single."

"Is it the room she's unhappy with?" I asked. I couldn't do anything to change it if I didn't know what the problem was.

She shook her head. "She didn't say anything to me. I thought she'd gotten into the vibe of the place. I haven't seen her so au natural for years." Emily was getting hyped up with the super-caffeinated drink and seemed close to tears. "She never liked any of my friends, thought all my boyfriends were uninteresting and fussed when I wouldn't major in computer science in college."

It was turning into a therapy session and she wanted a sympathetic ear. The best I could so was to listen and reassure her she was right in what she'd tried to do and that her intentions were good. In the midst of it all, I realized that I'd forgotten to call my mother as promised. I didn't want to cut Emily off, but when it got to the point that she was starting to repeat how the weekend hadn't turned out the way she hoped, I needed to wind it up. When she took a breath, I stepped in.

"You had the best of intentions. That's all you could do. And about the other stuff, you have to live your own life, not one to please your mother." I felt the chills as I said it because it was true for me, too.

She reached over and hugged me. "Thank you. I feel better. You're right. I did have good intentions." She went off to take a walk on the beach and clear her head after our conversation and I went home to face calling my mother.

Despite the whole pep talk I'd given Emily, I fell into the old trap and reacted to my mother's sigh when she said how worried she'd been when I didn't respond to her messages.

"I had so many last-minute things to do for this retreat. It's more complicated than the others I've put on. I explained the mystery game, leaving out a lot of details, like that Sammy had played the corpse, or that there had been a real one. "I got a different sort of group this time, and I had to bake some things for the afternoon tea."

"I'm sure it was all very important," my mother said with that sound in her voice that was supposed to remind me that her job was saving lives and yet she'd still had time to be concerned about me.

I considered if I should ask her about how hard it was to electrocute someone, but she'd already told me that she didn't like to talk about killing people when her job was to keep them alive.

"As long as you're all right," she said finally. "And you're happy with your life." The hidden message was that what I was doing didn't measure up to her expectations. But I'd grown up enough to let it go and only wished her a good day before signing off.

Julius followed me to the door and offered a plaintive meow and I couldn't resist and gave him some stink fish. If only everyone was so easy to please.

Chapter 25

I went back across the street and onto the Vista Del Mar grounds. It still amazed me how the surroundings changed just from walking through those stone pillars. My house was on the edge of town and the street was more rustic than those closer to the heart of Cadbury, but even with front "lawns" that were native plants (weeds) or ivy, the yards had a sense of order.

The Vista Del Mar grounds had a wild untamed feeling, as though the plants, trees and wildlife were in charge. There were no mowed lawns, but tall dry grasses and scruffy plants. Trees had foliage shaped by the wind and deer walked through as if the people were the invaders.

I went straight to our meeting room and had barely walked in when Crystal arrived with Cory. She'd driven her son in for his shift and I greeted the two of them. She had stayed with the boho look of a gauzy dress in shades of purple over the leggings and a long-sleeve black shirt. We'd come up with a uniform for Cory of black jeans with a silver buttoned vest and a pinned-on name tag.

He was all arms and legs and reminded me of a dangling spider somehow. Eventually, his body parts would catch up with each other and be in the right proportions.

"What happened?" he said in a disgruntled voice. "I thought people were supposed to question me about what I knew about the magician's murder." His mouth was almost in a pout. "I was all set with my story and nobody even asked."

I felt bad for him. He'd been so enthusiastic about being part of the whole thing and it had all fizzled. "I'm afraid the group turned out not to be so excited about following the clues because of something that happened."

"You mean the man in room 220?" he said, and I nodded. I had been purposely vague in case he'd didn't know about Gary Moser.

"I thought you might have been kept out of it," I said.

"No way. I had to help Mr. St. John keep everything quiet. We got the cops to keep their cars on the street so the guests wouldn't see them. It was my job to stand guard outside the room where the man was killed to make sure no one went in until they, uh, removed the body and they got through with the room," he stammered.

"You were right in the middle of it then," I said. "Did you notice anything interesting?"

"Because of your whole mystery thing, I was thinking about evidence and clues." He looked at his mother and she encouraged him to continue. "That guy was kind of weird. He seemed to be watching everybody. Even the people who worked here. He seemed most interested in one of the guests and even asked me if I'd seen her with anybody."

"Then my question is which guest, and did you see her with anybody?" He got another okay from his mother before he continued.

"I don't exactly know her name, but she always wore fancy sweat stuff and a baseball cap. I saw her once without it . . ." He closed his eyes and shook his head. "She looked bad."

"What do you mean?" I asked.

"Her face was all puffy, like she'd been crying, and I think there were some bruises. I offered to get her some ice." I looked at Crystal, thinking what a good job she'd done with him. It was so like him to always offer something extra. "She said she'd take care of it herself and seemed upset that I'd seen her face. She gave me a twenty and asked me to keep it to myself if anybody asked."

His smart watch made a noise. "I gotta go," Cory said. He started to give his mother a hug and then caught himself and turned it into a mock salute. "I have to help out in the café today. I'm hoping I learn how to make a killer cappuccino," he said, sounding enthusiastic. Seeing how happy he was being a part of Vista Del Mar made me glad that I'd uncovered his connection to the Delacortes. I was sure his great-grandfather would be proud to have him working there.

"Cory's a great kid," I said, watching him go.

"He is, isn't he. And so easy." She let out a heavy sigh. "I wish I could say the same for his sister."

We started talking about mother-daughter relationships. She knew about the issues with my mother. She got along better with her mother now, but there had been issues when she was younger and took off with a musician and then a lot of *I told you sos* when she showed up with two kids after her marriage fell apart.

"Even with this group," I said, "I got an earful this morning from Emily Van Ness about how much she wanted this weekend to please her mother and it seemed to have failed. She even arranged it so the destination was a big surprise."

"I feel for her," Crystal said. I did a quick survey of the room and was glad the fireplace was going strong enough to give off some warmth and the refreshment area was stocked with pots of hot coffee and hot water. There were still cookies from before.

Crystal looked over the table with me. A couple of them had left their tote bags with their projects. "Probably the guy with the shaved head," Crystal said. "He's a reluctant knitter, to put it mildly." She looked at me "And I'm guessing trouble for you."

"You are right on that." I shook my head, thinking of how hard it was to try to please them all. "This is such a different group than we usually get," I said. "And here they come." The sound of voices was getting louder as they came up the path.

Bruce Elliott was the first one in the door. "I can't wait to hear the information you've been dangling in front of us," he said, making it sound as though he believed whatever I had to say was going to be a disappointment.

"Before we get to that," I said, introducing Crystal. "She's only here for a limited time, so why don't we get started on your knitting and we can talk as you work."

I saw Bruce Elliott's eyes going skyward, but his wife nudged him and he kept quiet. It took a few minutes for the projects left behind to get to their right owners and the rest of them to take theirs out. When the needles started moving, Bruce Elliott did a loud throat clearing as a prompt for me to talk.

"It's good that we waited," I said. Bruce let out a groan, sensing another stall. "I actually have more to share," I said, ignoring Bruce's behavior. "To begin with, the man who died, Gary Moser, was a PI and a former cop." Even Bruce Elliott seemed surprised at the news.

"I wish I'd known when he crashed the afternoon tea," the shaved head man said. "I bet he had some good stories."

Mary Smith put her face in her hands. "I can't keep it in anymore. He came in with me. I had no idea he was a private investigator. He struck up a conversation with me and I mentioned the afternoon tea. He seemed very interested in it and I said I'd bring him in. I didn't know that someone was going to kill him," she said.

"Maybe you thought he just said that so he could spend time with you," Rose Wilburn said. "I know what it's like to be a woman on her own when it seems like everyone around you is part of a couple."

"It wasn't like that," Mary said. "He said he thought he'd left a book in the parlor." It seemed to me that she was protesting too much and I knew what I'd seen. It looked as if she had been pleased with his company.

"I think this whole line of discussion is a waste of time. What difference does it make why he came into the tea, though personally, I think it was about the food," Leslie Ackroyd said, looking at Mary. "No offense intended, but the story about him leaving a book in the room sounds like a line to me. And we all agree he took a hearty plate of food."

Mary Smith looked around at the group. "Whatever he was working on I'm sure had nothing to do with any of us." She turned to me. "Didn't you say you had more information to tell us?"

I would have liked to process what Mary had said, but the group was anxious to get on to more about Gary Moser. "I did see him have an angry exchange with a woman the night before all of you arrived. She seemed uncomfortable with his attention. At the time I thought he was hitting on her, but I didn't know he was a PI, which could have meant he was surveilling her and she figured it out. But it was in the Lodge and it might have only seemed as if he was watching her, when his real target was somebody else." I took a breath after getting all the words out.

"What about the woman?" Jenn Van Ness asked.

"Her name is Brook Tanner and she's been coming here regularly and told the desk clerk it was for a spiritual retreat. Yesterday a man came into the Lodge looking for someone who I now believe was her as I found out that he is her husband. As is the policy of Vista Del Mar, the assistant manager wouldn't give any information and asked him to leave. He got agitated and insisted the assistant manager pass along a message to the woman, telling her that she would get 'nada.'"

They were all listening intently now. "Late last night when I came here to drop off the muffins I'd baked for the café, she was coming back from somewhere. And her room was on the second floor of the building you all are staying in."

"Which is down the hall from where the PI was staying," Emily Van Ness said.

"That's correct," I said to Emily before turning to the rest of them. "There's one more thing. She seemed to need a lump of money for something. She tried to cash a check here. They didn't have enough cash on hand to cover it." I put up my hands. "There you have it. What do you think?"

"It's obvious," Victor Ackroyd said. "The PI was watching her and caught her with someone. She tried to pay him off, but couldn't because she couldn't get the cash, so she killed him. It never sounded like a premeditated crime to me. More like it was last-minute improvisation. If she was down the hall, she could have heard when he turned on the shower and gone to his room and done her dirty work."

"What was the man like?" Rose Wilbur asked.

"Wealthy and older. And he's been married multiple times," I said.

"Aha," Rose said. "It's just like the case on that podcast called

'The Lady Who Lost It all.' She'd signed a prenup that spelled out what she'd get in a divorce, but if she cheated on her husband, she'd get nothing, or *nada*." She gazed around at the group. "In her case, she killed her husband when he caught her with someone else, thinking she'd inherit everything and not have to worry about the prenup." Rose started to go into more detail how the plan had backfired, but Leslie Ackroyd interrupted her.

"We should stick to what's right in front of us. This Brook's husband must have been here trying to check up on the PI. It does seem pretty obvious that she got rid of the PI so he couldn't tell on her," Leslie said, agreeing with her husband.

"Then why haven't the cops arrested her?" Bruce Elliott said, putting his hand on his hip.

"I think they may have her in their crosshairs." I told them about the plainclothes cop having breakfast at a nearby table. "I'm not sure he was there watching her. Vista Del Mar has a generous policy of offering local police complimentary food, so he could have just been there for a free breakfast," I said. "As for why they haven't arrested her, just connecting the dots and thinking she's the one who did it isn't enough. There has to be evidence or they'd never be able to bring charges against the person."

"So, you're saying we have to get the evidence that she did it and present it to the police," Sandra Elliott said.

"That's not at all what I was saying." I pictured them trying to find a way to corner her and Lieutenant Borgnine getting wind of what they were doing. "The reason I told you was for you to see what you came up with given the clues."

"That seems like a waste of our brainpower," Bruce Elliott said.

"That is, if Brook is the real murderer. But what if it's not her. Even if the cops have their eye on her, it wouldn't be the first time they were wrong. Just read my books and you'll see how my amateur sleuth/park ranger Nellie with the help of her mind-reading cat always know better." Milton Carruthers added a smile to make it seem like the last part was a joke and not another pitch for his mysteries. "What about the housekeeper. Think about it—she was there when we went in the room. She'd have access to those extension cords and I bet there's a hair dryer somewhere she could have grabbed. Then after she'd done it, she screamed," he said.

"That's very clever, Milton," Madeleine said.

They had all put on their detective hats and were doing just what I'd hoped—conjecturing but not taking action. The conversation continued as they offered other possibilities.

"The housekeeper?" Victor Ackroyd said. "Isn't that a little too much like the butler did it. What would be her motive?"

"Maybe he showed up naked and tried to force himself on her," Rose Wilburn said. "It's too bad that the housekeeper isn't Jane, the one who's part of our game. Then we could have interrogated her as if we were asking about the dead magician and slipped in some questions about the actual corpse."

"I think the PI could have been watching someone else and that woman just imagined it because she felt guilty about something," Leslie Ackroyd said.

"You're right. By assuming that woman is the killer, we could be missing an opportunity to come up with other suspects. What if he was watching someone else entirely. Maybe one of us. Or it could have had nothing to do with who he was watching," Emily Van Ness said.

I was going to stay out of it and let them have their fun, but I couldn't help myself and brought up the group in the red shirts. "The victim seemed to know some of them," I said, remembering how after Brook Tanner had made her comment to him, one of the red-shirted men had suggested they get a beer. "The person in the red shirt seemed to know what Moser did because he made a comment like *you probably get a lot of that*, meaning someone telling him to back off. The people in the shirts are insurance claims adjusters. I know from my time working for a PI that they do a lot of work with insurance companies. Maybe he was on a job for them."

"That seems like a stretch. It's most likely that woman, Brook Tanner," Victor Ackroyd said.

"What now?" Rose Wilburn said.

"Let the cops do their thing," I said. "And you could go back to checking out the clues still there for the murder game."

"I vote for that," Jenn Van Ness said after raising her hand. "We don't have that much time left. Just this afternoon and then there's the event in Hummingbird Hall tonight. I just want to have fun," she said.

"I agree with my mother," Emily added. I understood she was trying to do what she could to make the weekend into something good for her mother.

"That would seem pretty dull after talking about a real crime," Victor Ackroyd said.

I'd noticed that Crystal seemed a little agitated and was looking at the knitting hanging off their needles. I followed her gaze, and to say they were a mess was an understatement. Except, of course, for Sandra Elliott, and I was sure she could do a perfect knit and purl combination in the midst of a hurricane.

"I hate to say this, but will you please all look at your work," my yarn consultant said. It took a moment for them to transition from talking about murder to what they were doing with their hands. Once they looked down they all let out a sigh of dismay in unison. Everyone but Sandra Elliott was holding a jumble of stitches that no way resembled anything that could be turned into a hand warmer.

"I guess talking and knitting wasn't such a good idea," Crystal said. I followed behind her as she walked around the table examining their work one by one. The simple repeat of two knit stitches and two purl stitches had gotten totally messed up. Crystal turned back to me with a sorrowful look. "It would take forever for me to fix the mistakes. I'm afraid the only prognosis for everyone but Sandra is to rip out and start again."

There were a lot of unhappy sounds. The loudest was from Bruce Elliott. "It was hard enough getting this far. But starting again—no way," he complained.

Crystal took back the floor. "I wish I could come back in the afternoon to help you, but I have to be in the shop." She handed Victor's work back to him. "But if you want you can all come to Cadbury Yarn. We have a nice table for social knitting. You can look at our yarn and I can help each of you to get your work straightened out."

"An outing would be nice," Madeleine said. "I'd love to have Milton see our wonderful town. And all of you, too," she hastily added.

If it made Madeleine happy, it was good with me and I told them I'd arrange for transportation.

When Crystal left, the group broke up and we agreed to meet outside the Lodge after lunch. I stayed behind to clear off the table. And then I went next door to check on the murder scene. The room was dimly lit with the only light coming in through a window that looked out on a small fenced-in area. It looked as though everything was as it had been once the "body" was moved and the chalk outline had replaced Sammy's shape. I felt bad at the way things had turned out. Maybe if there hadn't been a real murder they wouldn't have lost interest. I flipped on the lights and moved into the room to get a better look. Something had been dropped into the chalk outline. I assumed that one of the clues we'd left had migrated into the spot. When I got close enough to see exactly what it was, I felt the hair on the back of my neck stand up. It was a photograph, and even from a distance I recognized it as one of me. Something red had been dribbled on it and it was pierced in the vicinity of my heart with a tiny plastic sword. The kind that was used as a cocktail stirrer. I didn't want to pick up the photograph, as though the red stuff might be caustic. Instead, I leaned over studying it. I could tell by the clothing and background that it had been taken that morning in the dining hall.

I was considering what to do with it when I felt someone come up behind me and grab me.

Chapter 26

My instincts kicked in and I used my elbows to push away the intruder. I heard an *umph* sound, and as I twirled around expecting to free myself, something happened and I ended up on the floor in a locked position so I couldn't move. "What are you doing here?" I asked, looking up at Dane, and he laughed.

"I came by to see how things were going. But I certainly learned my lesson, no more unannounced affectionate moves," he said, releasing me. I thanked him for giving me a soft landing. Then he critiqued my moves as he helped me up. "You almost had it. But you hesitated and gave me an opportunity. You need to practice with the kids some more." He stopped and grinned. "Or maybe not. Then maybe it'll be me who ends up on the floor." He looked down at the chalk outline. "What was so interesting?"

I pointed to the picture. He had no qualms at picking it up and shook it, showing that the red stuff was dried. "It looks like somebody isn't happy with you." he said. "Maybe we should show it to Lieutenant Borgnine."

"No," I said, grabbing it. "It's probably just a sick joke from one of my people to show what they think of my clues."

"That's not very nice of them," he said. "Maybe I should have a talk with them as a professional crime fighter." He grinned at the title he'd given himself. "They should know how hard you worked on this."

"That's gallant of you, but no. I fight my own battles. I still believe I can turn this around." I told him about the upcoming outing and time at Cadbury Yarn. "It might help if they see some progress on their knitting." Then I remembered that he'd been kept out of the loop for fear he'd tell me something, which seemed pointless now. "I better bring you up to speed," I said.

"This is just weird. You giving me information. I'm not sure my ego can take it." He grinned to let me know he wasn't serious and then asked for the download. I told him all about Gary Moser being a PI and ex-cop, along with Brook Tanner's story. I added other possibilities for Moser's killer, but he agreed with Victor Ackroyd and thought in this case the obvious was true. He was also relieved that I'd managed to keep my people out of the investigation. "If we think it's her, I'm sure Borgnine knows it, too." He looked at the photo again. "This could be some kind of threat. Let me help you check it out."

"I'm sure it's nothing," I said

"At least let's go to the beach and I can teach you some better moves." I agreed, and we left the photo where it had been and crossed through the grounds to the soft white sand. It was supposed to be karate, but it turned into a lot of laughing and rolling around in the sand.

"I'm afraid my karate moves are like my flirting," I said, doing my bad version of batting my eyelashes. He started to laugh, and I took the opportunity to grab his arm and flip him.

He looked up from the ground and gave me a thumbs-up. "Pretty clever. Chalk one up for you."

I'd made light of the whole picture thing to him, but I was concerned. Was it somebody in my group as I'd said or was it somebody who knew I'd been gathering information? I waited until he'd left, and after I'd arranged for the transportation to take my people into town, before I did a little checking around. There was no cell service, but the cameras on everyone's phones still worked. I could only narrow it down to someone who'd been in the dining hall for breakfast which eliminated nobody. Even Cloris and Kevin St. John had come in while I was there. Then there was the question of how they'd gotten a print of the photo.

It didn't take much checking to find out there was a photo printer in the gift shop. But when I asked the cashier, she said there had been a lot of people using it and she merely took the money and gave them a code. I tracked down the plastic sword to the café, where Bob used them to spear lemon slices. There was always a plate of them left on the counter.

All of which meant it could be anybody. And I'd run out of time to think about it now.

• • •

The original plan had been for the retreat group to conclude solving the set-up crime on Saturday afternoon and then celebrate with a special event put on by Vista Del Mar. The events varied according to what sort of guests were staying at the hotel and conference center, and particularly what groups were having meetings or retreats. Because Madeleine was so involved with our retreat, Kevin St. John had planned something he thought would please her. The schedule called it a Tea Dance, though it was being held in the early evening instead of the afternoon. It promised a "tea" sort of meal and an evening of tangos, waltzes, foxtrots and cha-chas with dance lessons included.

Getting them off the grounds for the afternoon seemed like a good way to entertain them and get them to focus on their knitting, since we'd made a point that they'd finish at least one hand warmer during the weekend. It would also give them a chance to see downtown Cadbury. I'd lived most of my life in Chicago, where the downtown was an area of interesting tall buildings draped along the lakefront. My parents lived in a downtown high-rise that was part of it all and had a mesmerizing view of the lake. Downtown Cadbury might not have a fabulous skyline, but it did have its own charm. If nothing else, it would be a change of scenery for my group.

Lieutenant Borgnine was coming out of the Lodge as I stopped in the driveway next to the dark wood building to wait for the van. I knew he'd been on the grounds, but I hadn't had any exchanges with him since he'd gotten statements from my group. There was a hint of discomfort behind his gruff expression.

"Ms. Feldstein," he said with a nod of his head as a greeting. He saw the van drive up and stop next to me. "Taking your group somewhere?"

I explained the trip to the yarn store and he seemed pleased. "Good. No chance your 'detectives' will interfere then."

"Interfere with what? Are you going to make an arrest?" I said, trying not to sound too interested. I really wanted to share everything that I'd observed. I thought it would show we were both on the same page, but then I rethought it and decided to keep quiet. Let him have this one completely on his own.

He gave me a look as if I'd asked an absurd question. "A good cop never shows their hand," he said finally. Then he wanted to know how long my group would be gone. He nodded when I told him and I gathered it would mean they would miss the action. I wondered if I should add that I'd gone out of my way to keep my people from interfering with his investigation to get some points with him, but decided it was in my best interest to keep quiet.

When he saw the Elliotts approaching, he made a quick exit. Unfortunately, not fast enough for them not to see that he'd been talking to me.

"What did the cop want," Bruce Elliott said.

"He just wanted to know where we were going," I answered, which was the truth. I wasn't going to add the rest. They'd never go on the trip then. For once I actually agreed with Borgnine. It was better if my group wasn't there when they made the arrest. I didn't expect them to have a SWAT team or a lot of guns drawn. Most likely he was aiming for the quiet part of the afternoon when there would be the fewest witnesses and it was least likely there'd be any trouble.

The rest of the group arrived and they all piled into the van. Madeleine seemed to be entranced by riding with the others since her usual mode of transportation was a golf cart. She had always driven herself, but lately had been using a driver at her sister's insistence. With all her new adventures, Madeleine had become a bit of a reckless driver—as much as she could be with the small battery-operated vehicle.

In the past, most of my groups had jumped on their phones the minute they got far enough away to get cell service, but this time only Rose Wilburn took her phone out and seemed to be frantically doing something. Her breathing seemed to change, as if she was relieved and in a panic at the same time. She had listed her occupation as working in administration at a private college in Santa Clara. Maybe there had been emergency texts from students.

Whatever it was, she stopped when the van pulled up next to the small bungalow that housed Cadbury Yarn. The colorful wind sock swirled in the breeze as the group trooped across the small front porch and went inside.

Crystal greeted everyone and led the way to a back area with an oval wood table surrounded by chairs. There wasn't enough space for all of them to sit at the main table, but there were a couple of small ones set up for two.

The mood of the group changed somehow in the new environment. Maybe it was being away from the brooding feeling of Vista Del Mar or being surrounded by all the cubbies of colorful yarn, but they all started to talk to each other. It was an odd situation. They'd spent a couple of days together and knew each other, but didn't know about each other. I thought the talking might also be a stall before they got to the knitting. Except Sandra Elliott, who was finishing her second hand warmer.

"You never told us what that's about," Bruce Elliott said, indicating Victor Ackroyd's walking stick. He turned to his wife and she nodded what seemed like an okay.

"We have a design business. We do offices and such. I was on-site in a house a company wanted to make an office and the floor gave way."

"I hope they had insurance," Bruce said.

"They do, but dealing with them has been a nightmare." He seemed about to go into detail, but Leslie gave his arm a tug and he stopped.

"Isn't that the way. You pay a fortune for insurance and then they don't want to pay when you have a claim," Bruce said. "I wanted to say a word or two to those guys in the red shirts. I've dealt with their company—even one of those guys. They call themselves claims adjusters. Ha, adjusters, how about find a way to pay as little as possible should be their title." Although Sandra tried to stop him, he went on about the printing business they owned and a pipe that had broken in the next storefront and damaged their place. There was a lot of damage to the business, and a long fight with the insurance company. Sandra kept trying to stop him from complaining, to no avail. He was worked up by the end and said he was going to confront all the adjusters at the tea dance and tell them what he thought.

Sandra reminded him that he hated dancing and had said he was going to skip it.

"That was before. Now I have a reason."

"The only insurance connection I have is dental insurance," Jenn Van Ness said. "My late husband was a dentist and I worked in his office."

"It was a waste of her talent," Emily said. She hadn't given up on trying to find a way to make her mother pleased with the weekend. Jenn seemed surprised by the comment. "Remember how when it was the two of us and you had your own business doing people's taxes?"

"You flatter me," Jenn said. "It was hardly genius work, but it kept us going."

Rose Wilburn was content to make arrangements of skeins of yarn and assorted tools and take pictures. Someone asked her what she did. "It's too boring to talk about," she said and took a scarf off a rack of ones for sale. She fiddled with it and stood up and took a photo looking down at it.

Madeleine and Milton Carruthers seemed in their own little cocoon at one of the smaller tables. They were deep in conversation and I wished I could hear what they were saying, but there was no way to eavesdrop without being obvious. Mary Smith had dropped her things on a chair and then gone off to look at all the yarn. Was she really that interested or was it a way to stay out of the getting-to-know-you that the rest of them were doing. I remembered how she'd reacted when I mentioned that she'd left out her occupation on her registration form. I wondered if she had some odious job that she didn't want to talk about. She was proper-looking with the blunt-cut white hair, but what if she was something like a butcher who spent their days hacking up the sides of cows.

As soon as there was a lull in the conversations, Crystal took over the floor. I noticed that Mary rushed to her seat. It was ridiculous, but after my crazy conjecture, I looked at her hands wondering if there was any residue of cow's blood.

"Sorry to tell you to do this, but you have to rip the guts out of your work." She picked up a random needle holding someone's knitting and slid the last row off the needle before giving the yarn a tug to take out the rest of them. But there was resistance, and when she looked down at the rows of knitting she saw that not only were they mangled but so tight they were like knots. With a snip she cut the mess free from the ball of yarn. "This might be a better way to go. And faster. There is more than enough yarn in the skein to make the hand warmers."

This time there was no talking as they worked. Crystal and I kept walking around the tables watching what they were doing. At the end of their time, they all had a nice amount of the first rectangle done.

"You can finish this one when you get back to Vista Del Mar before the Saturday night festivities," she said. "And then tomorrow in our grand finale workshop, I'll show you how to sew up the side and begin the next one. "Otherwise, you'll have to keep one hand in your pocket." She smiled to let them know it was supposed to be a joke. Even with her whimsical way of dressing, she wasn't good at delivering a punch line.

We finished faster than I'd expected. I didn't want to take everybody back early for fear they'd come in just as Lieutenant Borgnine was leading Brook Tanner out in handcuffs. Actually, I thought he'd probably be more discreet than that, but it still didn't seem like a good idea to arrive back when something was going down.

"How would you like some time to look around Cadbury?" I offered. I would have thought they'd been on a desert island with no stores by the way they all agreed and then took off to go shopping. I gave them advance warning that there wasn't a ye olde saltwater taffy shop or anything that sold cheesy souvenirs. The best they could do was the twenty-four-hour pharmacy that sold postcards.

While they scattered, I went to the pharmacy to make sure what I'd said was correct. It really had become like a general store since it was always open. Only the very back was dedicated to their supposed purpose. Inflatable rafts dangled from the ceiling. There were shelves of food items and paper goods. One aisle had water shoes and T-shirts with nothing written on them. I found the rack of postcards and felt vindicated and was going to leave when the clerk from the pharmacy section called out my name. That was life in a small town. Everybody knew your name and your business. I waited, expecting her to say something about Dane. He was a popular cop with a reputation for helping out, whether it was carrying in a heavy package or rounding up a stray dog. It made our relationship even harder. If they thought I broke his heart, they would never forgive me.

But it turned out to have nothing to do with Dane. After a few moments of small talk, she got to why she'd called me over. "We have a prescription for one of the guests," the clerk said. "Do you want to take it for them?"

When I saw the name on the bag in my hand, I dropped it with a squeal. It was for Brook Tanner and I was at a loss what to say. I didn't want to give away that she might need it delivered to the jail. I also didn't want to seem like a jerk for not agreeing to take it to her. I finally got an out when I saw it was for prescription painkillers. "Doesn't she have to sign for these?"

"You're right," she said with a regretful gesture. "Thanks for keeping me out of trouble."

It seemed like Brook had a corner on the trouble market. Did she have a pill problem, too?

I went to the cat sanctuary after that to wait for the group. It was a converted storefront that offered them for adoption and a place to visit with them. The front had pet supplies and the back was a sectioned-off open area to meet the felines. A particularly friendly ginger cat named Spice jumped in my lap and hung out with me. By the end of my time there, I wondered how Julius would feel about sharing his stink fish with a girlfriend.

It was still early when the group assembled and I stalled by taking them to my favorite coffee spot. Maggie was behind the counter and had a red bandana tied over her dark hair. We nodded greetings at each other and I pointed to a couple of tables in the back. Milton Carruthers went ahead and pushed them together while Bruce Elliott grabbed some extra chairs.

"This is on me," I said before asking for their orders. When I got to the counter, Maggie already had my cappuccino ready. She pointed out the empty basket where my muffins had been.

"We could really double the order. We keep selling out earlier and earlier." She smiled at me. "If you bake more, they will come."

Maggie always had a friendly smile and always wore something red like the bandana. It was how she dealt with an inner sadness from some losses in her life. I admired how the loss of her son and husband hadn't made her bitter, but instead made her want to give off warmth and cheer to all her customers. I filled her in on my retreat group and their mystery weekend that had gone kind of flat.

She sent me back to the table and said the drinks would be delivered. I heard Madeleine telling Milton that this was her favorite spot for coffee. He was leaning close to her and they seemed in their own little world. I did my best to keep them part of the group by getting her to talk about all the different architectural styles in the buildings along the main street.

They were close to finishing up when I noticed someone come in.

She looked familiar but I couldn't place from where. It was like when you see your mail deliverer out of uniform. She saw me staring at her and came over to the table.

"It happens all the time," she said. "You're sure you know me, but you don't know from where." She smiled at the whole group before extending her hand to me. "I'm 'Jane,' the housekeeper in your mystery."

I apologized profusely, feeling embarrassed for not recognizing her, but then the housekeeper role had been generic and given to her at the last minute. Her name wasn't even really Jane.

She introduced herself by saying her real name was Page and explaining that she was taking acting classes at the same community college where Cloris was taking the hospitality classes. I saw Milton Carruthers's eyes light up as he invited her to join us. The others didn't get it, but I remembered that he'd been sorry that she wasn't the housekeeper who'd supposedly discovered Gary Moser, because then he could have interrogated her as part of the game and eased into the real event.

Had he forgotten who she was or was he down to the idea that talking to the wrong housekeeper was better than talking to none?

Leslie Ackroyd pulled over another chair and Page seemed happy to join the crowd. "I was waiting for you people to find me. I even hung out in the Lodge to be available for questioning."

I didn't want to tell her that her efforts had been wasted and they weren't interested, so instead I suggested they interrogate her now. The problem was that the only one who had really paid attention to the clues was Mary Smith, when she'd opened the envelope with copies of them before the staged murder. As the others hemmed and hawed, I prompted Mary about the receipt from the café.

"Yes," she said, as if trying to acclimate herself. "The magician had coffee with someone in the café. The receipt was for two drinks. The cups were there when he was found. One of them had a smear of lipstick." Mary's voice broke off after that, as she had forgotten the rest of it.

I tried to add some drama to my voice as I said, "It's a unique shade only made by Avalon Cosmetics and there's only one person who has a side gig selling them in town." And then I looked at Page. "Jane the housekeeper."

They all laughed and then Milton turned to her. "You must know the housekeeper who was there for the real murder," he said. Then he offered his theory that she could be the killer. Once he'd opened the door to that, they all started shooting questions and Page looked like she regretted stopping by.

She put up her hands. "I'm sure Laura had nothing to do with it. She was traumatized by the whole thing. The last I heard was that Mr. St. John had her look over a list of stuff that was in the room and then he gave her off until Tuesday."

"Well, we finally got to question somebody in your murder setup," Bruce Elliott said, looking at me. "Maybe Victor was right and this is your take on the thing about the butler always being the one who did it. And since there was no butler, it was the housekeeper who sold lipstick on the side."

Chapter 27

As the van pulled into Vista Del Mar, I looked ahead for any signs of trouble. There were no police cars or anything to indicate that there had been any commotion. It appeared that Lieutenant Borgnine's operation had gone smoothly. Kevin St. John had managed to keep Gary Moser's death under the radar and now had kept the arrest of the alleged killer quiet as well.

The grounds were generally peaceful at this time on a late Saturday afternoon. All the day's workshops, meetings or outings like ours were finished, and it was as though the heavy work of the weekend was done. The evening's entertainment was always the climax of the weekend. Sunday was only a partial day, meant for tying up ends and saying goodbye. I was actually glad that Page had stopped by the group. It had given an end to the staged mystery, even if they were wrong about who did it.

I took them all to our meeting room and got them to stick with their knitting. Talking was at a minimum, and between me and Sandra Elliott, we kept them all on track and they were close to finishing the rectangle for one of the hand warmers.

I released them and everyone scattered to get ready for the evening's activities. I took the opportunity to go home and crash for a few minutes before I changed into my evening attire. My group had brought dressy clothes for Saturday night, but I wondered about the rest of the guests. What would the cargo pants crew wear? And what about the insurance company bunch in their red shirts. I chuckled as I pictured them just adding a bow tie.

Dane was working so there was no chance he'd stop by and do stink fish duty. As I went through all the unwrapping as the cat moved around my ankles, I wondered what excuse Dane would come up with to stop by during the dance portion. My dancing was on the same level as my flirting and always good for a chuckle. This was likely to be even more comical since there were to be tango lessons. He'd come up with something like he heard someone was committing a crime by torturing the tango.

I wore my go-to simple black silk dress. It was cut on the bias and had a timeless look. I dressed up with a corsage of a red crocheted rose. When it came to shoes, I stuck to a pair of flats, thinking ahead to my potential dance partner's feet. It was a given that there'd be some stepped-on toes and the flats would do less damage. I finished it off with a long black sweater.

Julius tried to get another treat out of me before I left, but I shook my head as he went to the refrigerator and sat down. "No way, I'm not going to a dance wearing even a hint of eau de stink fish."

It seemed strange to be walking down the Vista Del Mar driveway dressed like this. I felt like I should break out in a tap dance or pose for a magazine cover shoot. I did do a twirl and laughed, feeling giddy about the evening ahead.

And then as I neared the Lodge something happened that didn't make sense.

The door opened and Brook Tanner, dressed in a gray track suit and the baseball cap, walked out holding a glass of red wine.

What? I stopped and watched as she crossed the driveway and headed up the hill to the Gulls building.

There was no way she could have been arrested and already gotten bailed out. Not on a late Saturday afternoon in Cadbury. Besides, she seemed far too calm. Had I missed something? The lieutenant certainly made it seem like an arrest was imminent.

Cloris would know what happened. I rushed inside, expecting to see her behind the registration counter, but Ned, the late-night clerk, was in her place. It seemed strange and I had a bad feeling. With everything going on that evening, there was no way that she would take it off. Ned was dealing with a couple who seemed to be just checking in and I waited until he finished before approaching him.

"Where's Cloris?" I said as soon as he looked up. His expression changed from friendly host to wary and guarded as he checked the area. Then he leaned close and dropped his voice.

"Didn't you hear?" he said. "What a shocker. Lieutenant Borgnine arrested her for the murder of that guy in the Sand and Sea building."

I heard the words but they didn't register. "What?" I said a little too loudly.

"I know, everybody was stunned when the lieutenant came in here with a couple of uniforms." He shook his head. "I can't believe she did it."

"She probably hasn't even been charged yet. Haven't you heard about innocent till proven guilty," I said.

"They wouldn't have arrested her if they didn't have evidence." He shrugged. "But I guess you just never know who somebody really is."

"You're saying that she was arrested for the murder of Gary Moser?" I said, still in disbelief.

"Yeah, that's the name I heard." His attention was distracted as some people came into the Lodge and crossed the front on their way to the café. Ned put his fingers to his lips as a warning to stop talking. He waited until they'd gone into the café to say anything. "Mr. St. John is insistent that everything go on as planned and that nobody brings it up to the guests. We aren't really even supposed to talk about it among ourselves, but you asked directly." Another couple came back into the cavernous room holding glasses of wine and looking for a place to sit.

"Sorry, but that's all I can say. I have to be ready to handle whatever comes up," he said, stepping back from the counter and giving the meeting area a once-over.

My mind was a blank as I went outside. It didn't seem to make any sense. I was still in a fog when I saw the Blue Door van drive by and park next to Hummingbird Hall. I followed the path and caught up with Lucinda as she got out of the van.

She was wearing the black uniform and touched the peaked hat. "This will be one of the last times for this. It's been fun." She sounded a little nostalgic and looked at me for confirmation. As soon as she saw my face her expression changed to concern.

"What's wrong? Did something happen?" She came up to me and put her arm around me. I told her what I'd just heard and she was stunned.

"Cloris? That's crazy. What evidence could they have?"

"I have no idea. I just know that I have to do something." I looked at the van and the door to the dark wood building.

"Don't worry about the setup," she said. "I can do it myself, and there's always Cory if I need help." As she spoke the dark-haired gangly teen came out of the building.

I thanked her and took off back to my place and got in the Mini Cooper. I was on autopilot all the way to the Cadbury police station, and as soon as I'd parked I rushed into the lobby. The officer in charge was behind a glass window and I could tell by his expression that he recognized me. Not by name, but as Dane's girlfriend. I thought it might give me some leverage when I said I wanted to speak with Cloris.

There was no leverage. As soon as he got a negative to his question as to whether I was her lawyer, he gave me a flat-out no.

I went back outside and paced up and down on the sidewalk in front of the windowless red brick building. Once again it came back to me that I didn't know anything about Cloris's life. She seemed as dedicated to Vista Del Mar as Kevin St. John was. It was their life, or so it seemed.

A cruiser went by on the street and stopped so abruptly at the curb that the brakes squealed.

"What's the matter?" Dane said as he jogged toward me. I told him the condensed version of what had happened. "I thought I'd be able to talk to Cloris," I said. "It turns out that being your girlfriend didn't help. I endured all that ribbing from them for nothing."

"Sorry. I thought being connected to me would carry more clout," he teased, and then he got serious. "You know I'd sneak you in if there was a way, but we all might end up in the cell with her." He looked at the police station. "Our entrance is in the back. Let me go in and see if I can talk to her."

He went to the cruiser to pull it in the parking lot and I went back to pacing.

His expression was serious when he returned, which made me feel even more uneasy. He took me in the front door and waved at the officer I'd dealt with before. There was a buzzing sound of a door unlocking and Dane took me back into the inner area. "The desk officer is letting me take you to the break room. I had to give him a story that I thought you were going to faint. Lucky for you I didn't let him call the paramedics."

The room was harshly lit and had a coffee pot with a brew that smelled so strong it had probably been reduced to a syrup. There were a couple of folding chairs and one well-worn easy chair. Nobody would accuse them of having ye olde police station. There was nothing folksy or inviting about it. I declined the coffee, but since he'd given the story I was faint, he insisted that I sit in the more comfortable chair and at least hold a glass of water. "We have to keep up the optics," he said. He gave my face another once-over to be sure the story wasn't true. "You're a trooper," he said.

He pulled the folding chair up next to me and talked in a low voice, keeping his eye on the door. "I saw the paperwork about the arrest," he said. "A piece of paper with her name on it was found in Moser's things. Lieutenant Borgnine did some checking on cases that Moser'd worked when he was a cop. Even when they retire, some cops have cases that stuck with them or cold ones that weren't cleared. When Moser was a cop, he arrested her for passing bad checks. She was just a teenager and did six months. When Lieutenant Borgnine checked with Kevin St. John, there was nothing on her application disclosing that. The lieutenant surmised that Moser had confronted her and threatened to tell the manager."

"And she killed him in a panic," I said and Dane nodded.

"Borgnine asked around and it seems to be common knowledge that Kevin St. John didn't like her being assistant manager or the power she had because of her relationship with the Delacorte family and was looking for something to discredit her so he could fire her and justify it to them."

"The 'power' she has is based on her doing a great job," I said.

He put up his hands. "Hey, I'm not the jury," he said. "I talked to her for a few moments and she's very upset. She didn't deny anything about the bad checks, but she claims that Gary Moser remembered her and was glad to see that she'd cleaned up her life. They never even discussed whether she'd told the manager about her past life." He checked the area again for any eavesdroppers. "She wanted me to apologize to you for not telling you she knew Gary Moser. And," he said with a sigh, "she asked if you'd work your magic and find the killer, like tonight."

"Tonight. That's in a few hours."

"You're a victim of your success," he said, squeezing my shoulder affectionately. Then he stood up and hustled me out of there. He held open the door to the lobby. "Good luck. I'll try to come by later. Maybe we can catch a dance."

"As if my mind is really on dancing," I said, blowing my breath out as I went out.

As soon as I got in my car, I called Frank.

"It's Saturday night, Feldstein. Are you turning into one of those all work and no play people? Whatever it is, make it quick. I have a dinner date. She's cooking and I don't want to keep her waiting"

"It sounds serious," I said, and he let out a chortle and then cut it off.

"If you're just calling about my social life, can we do it another time?" he said.

"That's not why I called and believe me, we need to talk now." I brought him up to speed on everything with Cloris and that she'd dropped it on me to find the real killer."

"What happened to Brook Tanner? Wasn't she the one?"

"That's what I thought and I thought that the lieutenant thought," I said in a tongue twister.

"Are you sure it isn't Cloris?" Frank said. "She kept her past a secret from you. Maybe there's more."

"I understand why she didn't tell me. It was in the past and she had moved on."

"By the way, he wouldn't have been the first PI to have an attachment to cases from when he was a cop." I could hear him fidgeting around and he finally said he was putting on some cologne. "This is the last thing I have to say. You probably have more information than you realize. You just need to put it in the right order."

And then he was gone.

I formulated a plan as I drove back. I would do what I was supposed to for the tea dance and light meal and hope the puzzle pieces put themselves in order.

Chapter 28

It was just getting dark when I got back to the grounds. I rushed to Hummingbird Hall to try to catch up on what I'd missed. Lucinda and Cory were just finishing arranging the platters of finger food. It had started out to be an afternoon tea, but then became more like a supper. We'd dumped the playbook of typical tea food of cucumber sandwiches and such, instead going more with a California theme. There were rounds of polenta with dabs of marinara sauce topped with tiny pieces of fresh mozzarella. The chef had made some sushi rolls with shrimp salad and cucumber. For the vegans there was hummus with olive tapenade and guacamole and a selection of chips. And Madeleine got her wish of Welsh rarebit. There were more of the delicious sour cream biscuits I'd made. Lucinda had made up a tray with the lemon bars and cookies. In addition to the tea and coffee, there was punch with ginger ale, frozen strawberries and a block of orange sherbet.

"Any progress?" Lucinda asked when I joined her next to the table.

I shook my head and told her what Cloris had said about finding the real killer. "It seems obvious that it's really Brook Tanner like we all thought. But I'd have to have some evidence to get Lieutenant Borgnine to change his mind."

"Hold that thought," Lucinda said. "Maybe we can figure something out. But first I have to call Tag to check on him. I left two servers to help him while I'm here. But he doesn't take anything out of the routine very well." When she was gone, I turned to Cory, who was lining cups around the punch bowl. I thanked him for taking my place.

"You know I move around to all different jobs. I'm not a porter tonight," he said, showing off his tuxedo. "I'm a dance partner for the single ladies." He looked very James Bond in the formal suit with the wired earpiece.

"Didn't you say that you were given the job of standing guard outside Gary Moser's room to make sure no one wandered in by mistake?"

"That was me. I'm the one the cops gave the list to when they were done," he said.

"List?" I asked, not sure what he meant.

"They left a list of everything they'd removed as evidence," he said. I had no idea if it would help me get something on Brook Tanner, but I was curious what they'd taken.

"I don't suppose you remember what was on it," I asked.

"Absolutely," he said. "I memorized it. I don't know why they took the shower curtain but left some of the other stuff in the room," he said with a shrug. He began to reel off everything they had taken. Nothing he said stood out and I was somewhat distracted as the guests started coming in.

Hummingbird Hall was used as an auditorium when rows of seats were brought in and placed facing the stage, or like that night used as a dance floor when the space was left clear. The design was like the Lodge with an open framework, but was different in that there were alcoves on either side and the back. We'd taken up one of the side alcoves for the food presentation, leaving the rest of the hall open for dancing.

It didn't exactly go along with my concept of a tea dance, but Kevin St. John had hired a DJ who also gave dance lessons. He was set up on the stage at the front, and the tall man dressed in black leather pants and a shiny black shirt seemed to be sizing up the crowd as they came in.

Lucinda returned with a roll of her eyes when I asked about Tag. She stationed herself next to me and we both had the same idea. We wanted to see what everybody was wearing.

"You don't have to worry about Brook Tanner making a run for it," Lucinda said. "She's in the café hanging out with the clerk and the barista. She must be skipping the dance.

"Now that Cloris was arrested, she probably thinks she's home free," I said. I nudged Lucinda as some of the cargo pants crowd came in.

"It looks like they put on fresh T-shirts," she said. A few of the women had changed into bright-colored gauzy skirts. I was absolutely on target about the insurance group. They had all added bow ties to the red shirts—even the few women in their group.

And then my people began to come in and Lucinda offered a running commentary. She thought Madeleine nailed it with a black crepe dress with sequins around the shoulders. Her cloche hat with a peacock feather was the cherry on the sundae. We both thought that Milton Carruthers looked dapper in his white dinner jacket.

"I love that," Lucinda said as Emily Van Ness came in wearing a long maroon dress that appeared to have shoulder pads. She had even sprinkled some glitter in her hair. Jenn Van Ness was just behind her wearing wide-leg black pants and a long tunic with a sequin trim. She'd done a whole number with her makeup that Lucinda liked, but when it came to the snood she wore on her head, Lucinda gave it a thumbs-down. "What happened to that beautiful hairstyle she had when she arrived?"

"Will you look at that," I said and pointed out Leslie Ackroyd's dress.

"I know that dress," Lucinda said in an excited voice. "It's contemporary Ralph Lauren but has the look of another time." She went on effusing over the crinkly floral dress that had a high neck and mutton sleeves with a blouson top.

"Your dress is perfect," Lucinda said as Leslie and Victor Ackroyd stopped by the table. She smiled at the compliment.

"That's what I thought too when I saw it in the Ralph Lauren shop. It was described as being a nod to the Belle Epoque era." She did a twirl to show it off.

Victor was looking ahead to the activity in the room. "There won't be any dancing for me." He had a disgruntled expression as he leaned heavily on the walking stick. Cory stepped forward and said he'd be making himself available as a partner, and they both chuckled at his courtly manner.

Mary Smith and Rose Wilburn came in with Kevin St. John. I wanted to grab him by the lapels of his black suit and yell at him for what he'd done to Cloris, but restrained myself, knowing it wouldn't help. The best I could do was tell the two lone women that the manager would be acting as a dancing partner at large. He heard me and was forced to agree.

Bruce Elliott had kept it simple and just wore a blue dress shirt over gray slacks. He walked in and looked around at the setup and then he saw some of the insurance people in their red shirts. He muttered something that sounded angry about a refused claim. "That's it. I'm going to tell them what I think."

Sandra Elliott tried to grab his arm and hold him back, but he released himself from her grasp and went across the room. Just as I was wondering if I should be ready to intercede, Tag showed up dressed in a tuxedo. Lucinda was shocked and he stated that he couldn't work with the two servers who were supposed to help him and he'd left them in charge.

He looked to the table and the stack of plates. "Are those from the Blue Door? Did you bring a checklist?" He turned to me. "You know she lost a cup." Lucinda was rolling her eyes.

The DJ started the music and announced that it was a foxtrot. My mind went to Cloris's request that I get the goods on the real killer that night. It felt a little impossible. Frank's thought that the clues were probably all there echoed in my mind. *But I still had to find them.* With all this commotion how was I going to figure out anything?

"Ms. Feldstein, you should really get out on the dance floor as an example. It'll help the rest of them get into the swing of it," Kevin St. John said. Cory heard him and offered his arm.

I was already apologizing for stepping on his feet as we began to do the foxtrot. He had the steps down and seemed unconcerned about protecting his toes. "I came prepared," he said. "I learned all the

Knot a Game

dances the other day."

Cory asked me about the lost cup Tag had mentioned. I gave him the whole story while we moved around the dance floor and I looked out at the crowd.

"It has to be somewhere," Cory said. He offered to try to find it, but I told him to leave it be. I noticed that Bruce Elliott had been joined by some of the other guests and they were having what looked like an escalating conversation with some of the people in the red shirts. Cory continued on, going back to the evidence list, and I heard something that I'd missed before. I even asked him to repeat what he'd said, realizing that it might change everything.

When the dance was over, I told Cory I was going to check on something in case anyone asked where I was. I knew he wanted details, but I wasn't saying anything until I saw if the pieces fit.

The grounds were deserted with everyone at the dance.

The Lodge was empty and no one was even behind the counter. I peeked into the café and saw three people sitting at a table. Just as Lucinda had said, Brook Tanner was sitting with the desk clerk and the barista. At least I knew where she was and that she was out of the way. They didn't even look up as I slipped past the open door.

I tried to be silent as I went into one of the vintage phone booths and folded the door shut. I had to figure out all over again how to use the pay phone to call Frank. The phone rang for a long time and I realized he might not answer it because the caller ID probably said something like *pay phone*.

Finally, he answered. "This better not be a robocall," he said in a crusty voice.

I rushed to identify myself in a whisper.

"I can't hear you," he said. I took a chance and spoke a little louder, saying it was me.

"Feldstein?" He sounded surprised, and not happy surprised. "This better be like life or death. You got me just when we were getting to dessert, if you know what I mean."

197

Even if there had been time, I wouldn't have responded to his comment. I tried to blot out the mental image I had of the two of them cuddling in his recliner office chair.

"I need you to check something out for me," I said.

"You're kidding," he said, sounding gruff, and then he relented. "Okay, but only if I can do it quickly."

"I want to know about Gary Moser's old cases."

"Feldstein, not only would that take forever. I'd have to call in favors to get access. It would cost you months' worth of cookies."

I was feeling a little desperate and had another idea. "How about I give you a name and you do a search connecting it with Gary Moser and Santa Clara PD."

"Not bad, Feldstein. Of course, I'd come up with that if I'd had a minute." He was less optimistic when I said it was actually only a first name and an initial, but tried anyway.

"Bingo, or maybe I should say eureka," he said, and I held my breath as he read an old newspaper article. I asked what the person looked like and he gave me details. I told him about the missing cup.

"That's why he crashed the afternoon tea. He thought he recognized somebody and wanted to get something with their fingerprints. The cup wasn't on the list of evidence the cops took."

"And you think it's still in the room. Why don't you just tell the cops about it and stay out of trouble," Frank said.

"I can't chance looking like an idiot if I'm wrong and there is no cup. Everybody is busy and I'll be in and out in no time."

"Feldstein, you really ought to consider carrying if you're going to do stuff like this."

"Me, carry a gun? No way. My wits are my weapon." I heard him chortle at the thought.

Chapter 29

I slipped out of the phone booth and listened for a moment. The voices were still coming from the café, and as the saying went, the coast was clear. The door to the business area had been left open and it was easy to get to the space behind the massive wooden counter. I grabbed the spare key for the second-floor room and went out a back exit.

I got to the Sand and Sea building and went inside. The fireplace was glowing to a room of empty chairs. The police had finished with their investigation of the room, and Cory had said it had been left as is for the moment. There was no one watching me as I went to the second floor and down the dark hall, and I felt the adrenaline starting to pump through my system, kicking up my heartbeat and making my mouth go dry. The key turned easily and I was inside the room. It felt eerie as I turned on the light and saw the unmade bed and his duffel bag against the wall. The cord was gone, along with the appliance that had been attached to it, but even so, I didn't particularly want to look in the bathroom. With everybody busy at the dance, I didn't feel any need to rush and made a point to take some deep breaths to calm myself.

I checked around the room, figuring that if the cup was there, it would be in a paper bag to protect the fingerprints. Moser seemed to have liked candy. There was a candy wrapper and an open bag of gummy bears next to the bed and a jar of candy still in the bag from the gift shop on the dresser. I pulled open another bag on a table next to a lamp and found some toiletries. When I checked the table with the clock radio, I found a paper sack next to it. I wanted to high-five myself when I picked it up and opened it, exposing the cup. The cops must have thought it was just a souvenir and left it. It was a souvenir of sorts, as it had the fingerprints of someone from his past. I was considering if I should leave it and get Lieutenant Borgnine, or take it for safekeeping.

I felt the floor shift slightly, as if someone was coming down the hall. It could have been someone going to one of the other rooms on the floor or, I thought with a sinking feeling, someone was headed there. Just in case, I slipped into the closet. There was the sound of the door opening and then closing. I tried to flatten myself against the wall, willing myself invisible as I heard someone looking around the room. Was there a chance they would give up and leave?

Just when I thought my wish might have come true, the closet door opened and I found myself face-to-face with Jenn Van Ness. There was something icy about her expression, and I heard a click in her hand as a long blade flipped out from a handle. She had a can of something in her other hand.

"Where is it?" she demanded.

"Where's what?" I said.

"Please save me from the games. You know exactly what I mean. I heard all of that about a cup." She had me in a laser gaze as I looked at the bag on the dresser for a second and then at the bag next to the lamp.

"If you're going to be a detective, you shouldn't be so obvious." She started to go to the one on the dresser, but went to the bag next to the lamp first and looked inside. "Shampoo," she said, dropping it back on the table. Then she grabbed the other one.

"What do you think you know?" she asked. Her whole demeanor had changed and she wasn't the woman worried about being called a widow, she was desperate, ruthless maybe, and someone intent on surviving.

I was proud of what I'd figured out, but it was one of those times when it seemed better to be humble. "Nothing really," I said. "It is all just supposition. If the cup goes, there's nothing to connect you to Gary Moser's death. The cops already arrested somebody else."

"And you're saying that you wouldn't talk," she said.

"They wouldn't believe me anyway."

"Even so, why take chances." She went to the window and flung the bag out into the darkness. There was a thunk as it hit the ground and the sound of something breaking.

"So, we're good then." I made a move to leave, but she held the knife up, pointing it at me.

"I don't think so," she said. When she'd picked up the bag, she'd set down the can she'd had in her hand, but now she went to pick it up again.

"That housekeeper's closet has all kinds of goodies for getting rid of problems. The cord and this." I saw the can she was holding was a bug bomb.

The blade got close to me as she tried to push me into the tiny space. I resisted and the knife drew a little blood. "For heaven's sake, just move," she said, sounding impatient. She grabbed my arm just as there was a sound coming from the hall and the door flew open.

Madeleine, Milton and Cory rushed in, but by now Jenn had me in a hold with the knife at my throat as she moved us in front of the door, blocking their exit.

"Unhand her," Milton said, trying to sound authoritative.

"That's right," Madeleine said. "Unhand her."

"Really?" Jenn said to Milton. "That might work in one of your books, but not here." She waved the knife at them. "You can all get in the closet with her." She used the knife to get us all inside the small room.

She stopped in the doorway to the closet and was ready to arm the can. Then she kicked a doorstop in place outside the closet door so that when she shut it, the rubber stop would make it impossible to open from the inside. The four of us would be stuck in the small space with an aerosol of poison gas.

I looked down at the spot where the knife had cut my arm as blood oozed out. I rocked my head and I half closed my eyes. "I can't stand the sight of my own blood," I wailed, looking at Jenn. "I think I'm going to be sick." I lurched toward her, making retching sounds. She was trying to hold the knife, fend off any throw-up and arm the can at the same time. Something happened and the can began to spew a fine mist.

I made a move toward her, and before she could respond, I'd grabbed her arm and sent her flying in a flip toward the floor. It worked just as it had at the beach with Dane. Madeleine screamed as Jenn landed at her feet and the knife fell on the floor. Cory leapt into action, grabbing the spewing can as he ran to the window. It sailed out into the night. I had a hold on the woman on the ground. "Pretending I'm going to be sick gets them every time."

There was a rumble of footsteps from the hall and Lieutenant Borgnine and Kevin St. John rushed into the room. They looked at the three of them standing and me leaning on Jenn Van Ness as she laid on the ground.

"An explanation, please," Lieutenant Borgnine said to the group at large.

Jenn rushed to speak first. "She's gone crazy," Jenn said, trying to sit up. "I'm going to sue this place for being treated like this. She attacked me and dragged me in here. I was hoping those three would help." She looked to Madeleine, Milton and Cory. "She had some insane story about looking for a missing cup." She looked around the room from her vantage point. "There's no cup in here." She was trying to slide the knife under her so it would be out of sight.

Milton used the tip of his shoe to kick the knife away from her. "She was brandishing it at all of us," he said, indicating Jenn.

"She tried to get us all to go in the closet so she could poison us, but Casey used some martial arts to get her on the ground," Madeleine said. "She and Cory saved us all. He is definitely a Delacorte." She went to hug him. "It was all very exciting."

"New skill?" the lieutenant said, turning to me. "I bet I know who taught you."

"You can't punish him for teaching me self-defense," I said. "You should thank him, and us for springing into action."

"Before there are any kudos, how about you tell me the story."

"Her name is Jenn Van Ness or Jenn Peltier, if you go by one of her married names. Before that she had the same initial, but the *P* stood for Pomelo. She looked different in those days with white-blond hair and a bigger nose. Jennifer Pomelo kept the records for Sal "the Snake" Ruggio. Gary Moser had the case wrapped up for tax evasion, money laundering and fraud against Ruggio based on Jennifer's expected testimony. But then she disappeared before the trial. Ruggio walked, and Moser vowed to never stop looking for her. He was here working on some other case and he must have recognized her, but not been sure since she looked different. Since he couldn't be sure, he wanted to get something with her fingerprints so he could check them against the ones they had on file."

I walked over to the table with the clock radio and the paper sack next to it. I opened the top and showed the cup to him.

"But it was gone. I heard it break," Jenn said.

"You heard something break. It was a jar of candy. I faked you out and got you to grab the wrong paper sack. It just goes to show you that you should always double-check before you throw something out of the window."

Jenn sat up and let out a heavy sigh. "You have to understand, Ruggio's people would have killed me before I testified," Jenn said. "I had to vanish. I couldn't let Moser turn me in. Now, they'd go after me and my daughter. It was self-defense."

Borgnine shook his head. "That's not my call." He took her arm and helped her up. "You're under arrest for attacking her for starters." He pointed at the cut on my arm. "The district attorney will have to figure out the rest." He turned to me. "Do you need to go to the hospital or anything?"

"It stopped bleeding. Just a Band-Aid," I said.

"I'll have the officer bring a first aid kit when he comes for your statements."

"Statements?" the manager said. "I don't want a bunch of cruisers here." He looked at Madeleine. "Your sister is very concerned about our public persona. I think I have done a miraculous job keeping that murder under the radar. I don't want somebody writing a review of Vista Del Mar and talking about crimes and police."

"Is somebody writing a review?" I said.

"I heard someone on one of the pay phones. They said something about a deadline, a review and Cadbury."

"Did you see the person?" I asked.

He shook his head, as if I'd asked the most ridiculous question. "Of course not, how would that look if I heard someone was writing a review and I stuck my head in their face. I heard it as I was walking by.

"Let's not waste any more time," Kevin St. John said to the lieutenant. "You need to get to Hummingbird Hall. There's practically a gang fight."

As soon as a couple of uniforms arrived to take Jenn of the many last names away and seal the room, we all went back to Hummingbird Hall.

"See," Kevin St. John said, pointing to the dance floor. Then he glared at me and was about to say something, but he realized Madeleine was part of the entourage and instantly became more polite.

"What now?" the lieutenant said, eyeing the standoff going on between the red-shirted claims adjusters on one side and a group of guests including Bruce Elliott and Victor Ackroyd on the other. There were a lot of hostile stares and calling out of taunts as both sides seemed to be moving closer to the center, where something could erupt.

"Do something," Kevin St. John said. "We can't have our guests in a fistfight."

The DJ had been on a break and grabbed the microphone as he surveyed the groups closing in on the middle of the dance floor. "It looks like we have some trouble," the DJ said in a light tone of voice. "It happens with a lot of events we do. Weddings where the new in-laws are hostile. Birthday parties where people drink too much and old wounds reopen. But we've found a way to keep the peace that always works. A dance rumble.

"The rules are that you can get into each other's faces, but no touching. You can only use steps to express your hostility. We find the cha-cha works very well for this. At the end of the number, you might even shake hands."

The music came up loud with a throbbing cha-cha beat. The red shirts took up one side of the dance floor. Bruce Elliott, Victor Ackroyd, and the rest of their gang took up the other side.

It took some convincing, but the red shirts finally made the first move, doing cha-cha steps to push the others back. Bruce Elliott seemed the de facto leader and led the dance charge toward the red shirts, and they were up close in each other's faces waving their arms to the beat, almost touching each other. Victor was trying to dance with the walking stick, but after a moment, Leslie came out from the sidelines and took over for him.

She was really into it. Waving her arms and using her fingers to point at the red-shirted woman in front of her. The dance got more frenzied and the cha-cha became like an aggressive march toward an opponent.

The music got faster and then rose into a crescendo and ended. The dancing stopped and it seemed as if they'd all gotten a stitch in their sides and were breathing heavily. None of them had the energy left to be aggressive. They all made a rush to the punch bowl as the two groups mingled and conversations started. I got closer to hear what was being said.

The man in the red shirt that Bruce Elliott had been confronting with strident cha-cha moves was next to him and said something about only doing his job, but that he'd have another look. Bruce wiped his brow and touched the man on the back and then retracted it when it was all sweaty. "I get it, it wasn't personal."

It was a little more heated between Leslie Ackroyd and the red-shirted woman she had aimed her dance moves at. "Poor Victor is trying to get better and every time he can take a step without the walking stick, he feels good, but then worried that you people have someone watching him and that they will claim his injury is a fraud. We thought the PI who was here was watching him." I held my breath, waiting to see if Leslie would say what happened to Gary Moser, but she didn't. The woman took a step back and put her hands up.

"It's wasn't me," she said. "I don't know anything about your husband's case. But we do get a lot of people faking it to get paid. Since it's with our insurance company, I promise to look into it."

Not everyone was making up, but it did seem that the dance had dissolved their anger or they were just too drained to express it.

"It looks like you don't need me," Lieutenant Borgnine said. "Now, if we can take care of the rest of our business." While the dance continued, he took Madeleine, Milton Carruthers and Cory along with me back to the lobby of the Sand and Sea building where we could give our statements out of the public eye.

"This is so much more exciting than I imagined," Madeleine said. "Mrs. Maple got to be a real live detective."

"You were wonderful," Milton said. "The way you didn't panic when you saw the knife. It's certainly different dealing with a killer in real life. It's always orderly in my books. I get everybody together and Nellie points the finger at the guilty party with her cat's help and the killer gives up after that."

"My brother Edmund would be proud if he'd seen how you jumped into action," Madeleine said to Cory.

"I really did spring into action, didn't I," the gangly teen said.

"I'm glad you came along when you all did," I said.

"Mrs. Maple and Mr. Carruthers were looking for you," Cory said. "I was telling them that you'd gone off to check something and then I heard some noise coming through the walkie-talkie." He pointed to the earpiece. "The sound was not very clear, but it sounded like trouble."

I remembered that there had been a headset on the floor in Gary Moser's room, no doubt left by the housekeeper who had found him.

Lieutenant Borgnine looked like he wanted to tear out what little hair he still had as he listened to us. When he'd gotten our statements, I asked him about Cloris.

"She'll be released," he said.

"When?" I said.

He let out a weary sigh. "It's in the works."

"Why did you arrest her in the first place?" I demanded.

He gave me a look before he spoke. "She had a motive," he said, and then let out another weary sigh. "I knew it would never stick. Maybe now you see that murder isn't a game." He looked at me. "Not so much fun when someone is really arrested, is it?"

I knew it was best to just agree and I nodded. "Now then, I do have other things to take care of, like what to do about the woman's daughter." He handed me a bandage for my arm before he looked over our little group and said we were done and we could go back to the dance.

Chapter 30

Lucinda looked up when our little group walked in again. Surprisingly none of the four of us looked like we'd gone through a life-and-death struggle. If anything, Madeleine seemed to be glowing. We had only made a hasty appearance during the dance war, but now I owed her an explanation. M & M, as Madeleine and Milton started calling themselves, were anxious to get a dance in and went right to the open space.

Lucinda had given Tag the job of keeping the punch cups stacked up in threes. I leaned close to my friend to share all that had happened.

"You can tell Tag that I found his missing cup." Lucinda laughed and then looked stricken.

"Remember, I told him it got broken," she said. "He'll have a fit if he hears it showed up."

"It's probably just as well that you leave it be then. I think that cup is going to be tied up for a while." I told her everything, sparing no details.

"She's the one?" Lucinda said when I told her about Jenn. "Wow, who would have thought she had a secret life." She looked out at the crowd. Kevin St. John had found Emily Van Ness and was hustling her to the door. I saw a uniform waiting for her.

"They're probably taking her into protective custody," I said. I felt for her, remembering how she'd wanted so badly for her mother to enjoy the weekend. "She has to be in shock finding out who her mother really is and that she's now in danger."

"You really saved the day," Lucinda said.

"The good news is that I got Cloris off the hook, at least sort of. Thanks to Lieutenant Borgnine's antics, her secret is out and it may mean her job here."

Some people approached the table and Lucinda went to serve them some punch.

The music ended and a soothing waltz started. Cory came up to me and asked me to dance. "I'm glad to see you've recovered after what you did," I said and smiled. "I know you're supposed to circulate with the single ladies. I appreciate the offer, but if you want to save your feet, you'll pick someone else. Like her." I pointed out Rose Wilburn.

Cory agreed with a shrug and I watched as he asked her to dance. Her face lit up and they went out onto the floor. I wondered about Mary Smith, but she was talking to Tag as he arranged the cups. I would have loved to eavesdrop, but I felt like I had to keep an eye on things. I was still keyed up from the whole encounter with Jenn and finding it hard to get back to normal, let alone relax.

Just then Dane came in. He was in uniform and Cloris was with him. She looked undone, to put it mildly. Her eyes seemed swollen, probably from all the crying. Her bun had come loose and her usually crisp clothes seemed disheveled. But I'm sure I'd look even worse if I'd spent a day in jail. She rushed over and hugged me.

"How can I ever thank you?" She seemed to be tearing up. "I've made such a mess of things."

I was attempting to console her, giving her all the platitudes that things would look better after she got a good night's sleep. I saw Kevin St. John in my peripheral vision as he stopped next to us. I assumed he was coming to say something reassuring to Cloris, but he had an odd glint in his eye that made me uneasy.

"May I have the jacket, please," he said, holding out his hand. The words were polite enough, but there was something triumphant in his voice. She bowed her head as she slipped out of the blazer and handed it to him.

"You're firing her in the middle of the tea dance? I thought you were always trying to keep the dark side of things from the guests."

"Nobody is paying any attention," he said in an impatient tone. "She lied on her application, which is grounds for immediate dismissal."

"I'm sorry," I said, grasping her hand.

"Mr. St. John is right. I did lie and now I have to bear the consequences." He followed her as she walked to the exit.

Dane had watched it all, staying out of it. Now he put a hand on my shoulder. "You'll figure out a way to help her. You should feel good about what you did. You got her out of jail and off the hook. I didn't think there was any way that you'd lock things up so fast. A mob boss's accountant," he said, shaking his head in disbelief at the truth about Jenn Van Ness. The sympathetic tone turned into his teasing mode as he struck a cocky pose. "Though I suppose I deserve some of the credit. Who's the one who taught you how to flip someone."

"I wouldn't say taught me. More like did it to me and then I figured it out," I said, smiling at him. He had made me feel better and I was sure he was right. I would find a way to help Cloris.

"Didn't you promise me a dance," he said, looking at the dance floor and the couples gliding across it. He held out his hand.

"Are you sure your feet can take it?" I said.

He laughed and looked down. "I came prepared. These are cop shoes with steel toes."

We'd barely cruised around the floor once and the DJ announced the tango lessons. Dane put on a mock pout. "I wish I could stay for this, but Borgnine gave me a time limit and I have to go. And sorry, but I won't be making a surprise late-night visit. Because of the arrest and her daughter, the lieutenant said we need more security and gave me an extra shift." He looked back at all the people spread around the room and focused on some of my people.

"They don't know what happened. I'll sort it all out tomorrow," I said, feeling exhaustion sink in. "I've had all I can deal with for one day."

Chapter 31

When the phone rang Sunday morning, it felt like it was coming from someplace far away. With each ring it seemed a little closer, and finally I opened my eyes. I had managed to take off my dress and it was draped on a chair. I was still wearing my shoes though and was twisted in the covers. I hadn't had a drop of alcohol, but I felt like I had a hangover. Julius sensed I'd had a hard night and steered clear of me, sleeping cuddled in a chair.

Early Sunday morning phone calls were my mother's MO. I still wondered if she really didn't get the two-hour time difference or she figured it was a sure time to reach me. Either way, I hardly felt up for one of her calls. Maybe if I drank a pot of coffee first, I could handle our verbal dueling. I was going to let it go to voicemail, but reconsidered. Who knew what she would do if she thought I wasn't home at the crack of dawn on a Sunday morning.

I picked up the phone, croaked a hello, and expected to hear her voice. Hearing a male voice instead startled me and I sat up as the caller repeated the greeting.

"Frank?" I said, surprised.

"You sound horrible," he said. "Are you okay?"

"It's early here and no coffee yet," I said. "It's early even where you are." I saw the time on my watch. "It must have been an early night for you."

"Or I'm on my way home," he said. "A lot of women think PIs are sexy and romantic." I hadn't seen that side of him, but then I hadn't imagined that he would name his kitten Mittens.

I let out a yawn and stretched. Julius had opened his eyes and was watching me to see if I was going to the kitchen. "Irrespective of that, I'm assuming there's a reason for your call."

"Well, yeah, Feldstein, last time I talked to you, we figured out that woman in your retreat group did books for Sal Ruggio. I had to find out what happened."

"Oh, that," I said, faking nonchalance. Then I told him how it all went down.

"She was going to off you with a bug bomb in a closet?" he said. "Not how I'd like to go."

"Me, either," I said and told him what I'd done. He sounded impressed.

"Tell me again what it was that tipped you off it was her?" Frank asked. My mouth felt dry and I really needed a drink of something, but if I went to the kitchen, Julius would harass me for a snack. I decided to avoid it by staying put.

"It was her hair," I said. "When she arrived, she had this amazing hairstyle, smooth with perfect waves all the way down her shoulder. When I complimented her on her hair, she said it wasn't natural, that she had a tool that did it. Her daughter even commented on how much time her mother spent fussing with her hair and makeup.

"I didn't think much of it when her hair was all frizzy and pulled into a scrunchy the next morning. But it seemed odd when she had her hair shoved under a snood at the dance."

"Snood? Scrunchy? Please explain. I probably should know terms like that now that I, uh, am with someone."

I explained that a snood was a loose sort of mixture of a hat and scarf. As soon as I said how I'd used a scrunchy when I worked for him, he recognized that it was a decorated elastic hair tie. "The point is why would she have her hair under wraps? And then Cory—" I stopped to explain who he was before telling Frank about the evidence list of things they'd taken from Moser's room. "I'd heard the appliance called a hair dryer," I said. "But the list was specific and described it as a hair shaping tool."

"Good work," Feldstein. "And now you can enjoy your day. Didn't you say they have a special breakfast on Sunday?"

"Everything isn't exactly copasetic." I told him about Cloris losing her job, and that it was still weird about Brook Tanner. "I'd really like to know why the lieutenant backed off of her when she seemed like the most likely suspect."

"The answer to that is that he found a more likely suspect in Cloris, and then you found him an even better one. About Cloris's job, don't bother with the manager. He's on a power trip. You said he was looking to get rid of her, and he found a way. Go to where you have power."

"You mean the Delacortes?" I said. "I know they like her, but I'll still have to plead her case." I went back to Brook Tanner. "It's just curiosity now that I know she's not the one who did it. But I'd really like to know the missing pieces in her story. It seems like Moser never found a paramour and that he was getting impatient. She also might have paid him off." I untwisted the covers and the cold air began to revive me. "Maybe she really did come for a spiritual retreat," I said and Frank chortled.

"Nothing you've said about her sounds like that. She would have been chanting or meditating or something. Not wandering around aimlessly as if she was killing time," he said. "There really could be no guy. Also not a spiritual retreat."

"What then?"

"Feldstein, you got a lot of info there. See what you can figure out. If that's the end of your problems," he said, and I could tell he was getting ready to sign off.

"No, wait, there's something else. My group is going to have a fit when they hear I went ahead and caught the killer without them. It was supposed to be a mystery weekend."

"That's ridiculous. Your people are just fascinated by mysteries— they aren't like you, almost a real PI. They would have been like excess baggage. That woman might have succeeded in taking you all out with the bug bomb." He punctuated it with a laugh at the absurdity of the idea. "If I were you, I'd try to get them to solve that mystery you set up. It'll tie everything in a bow. They will be satisfied and your reputation will be saved."

"You view me as almost a PI," I said.

"Don't let it go to your head. But I've told you before that you have a lot of natural talent." He laughed. "And you're fearless or crazy. The woman had a switchblade."

"Frank, thank you. You've never been so generous with advice. How can I thank you?"

"You can never send too many cookies," he said.

I promised to ship off the first batch the next day.

. . .

Sunday breakfast was always extra sumptuous with waffles *and* pancakes, real maple syrup and a fruit bowl with all those berries that Bruce Elliott had complained were missing. I would have washed it all down with endless cups of coffee, but then I would have run into at least some of the group and been in the awkward position of having to tell them piecemeal about what happened. I wanted to tell them all at once during the last knitting workshop. So, I stayed home and had a bowl of slightly gummy instant oatmeal. At least the coffee was good.

There was another upside to my solitary breakfast. It gave me a chance to think, and something about Brook Tanner slipped back into my mind. I did a little checking and finally thought I had the answer to what she was really doing at Vista Del Mar.

Thanks to all the coffee and a hot shower, I was one hundred percent back by the time I went across the street. There was always a different feeling on Sunday mornings. It was as though people were already feeling nostalgic about their time there as they tied up loose ends and got ready to go back to the real world.

Crystal was waiting when I went to the meeting room. Her outfit alone was enough to make me smile. She'd worn another colorful dress over leggings and this time added a fascinator to her outfit. The tiny hat sat forward on her head and had stars and moons bopping up and down.

I began by apologizing for putting Cory in harm's way.

"Are you kidding? He loved being the hero. He told me that Madeleine had said something about him being a true Delacorte. How is he ever going to settle for a normal day at school?" she said with a laugh. She grew serious when she mentioned Cloris and said it was a shame.

"We all make mistakes," I said. "What makes the difference is if you find a way past them. I'm sure you know about that." She knew I was referring to her rock god ex.

"Jerk that Rixx turned out to be, I love my kids," she said. "And I have found a way not to repeat my bad judgment." She looked directly at me. "I know what you're trying to say. That Cloris deserves another chance. And you're hoping I can use my Delacorte heritage to influence the sisters. Of course I'll do it."

Our conversation was cut off when the group arrived. Bruce Elliott and the Ackroyds were still flying high from the dance rumble and I heard one of them say they had no idea the cha-cha could be such a menacing dance. "I got that guy to take another look at our case," Bruce Elliott said.

"It would be good if we didn't have to use our savings to pay for the damage to our store," Sandra Elliott said.

"They'll pay for all of it or get the other insurance company to do it," Bruce said. "When he heard that it was the neighboring store that caused the problem, he sure changed his tune."

"I got an apology," Victor Ackroyd said. "I don't know that anybody was actually watching me, but they said I didn't have to worry about easing off on the walking stick." He still had it next to him and said he wasn't ready to stop using it completely. "But it was nice to know that I don't have to worry that I look like a fraud when I don't use it."

When Madeleine and Milton Carruthers came in, they told me they hadn't shared anything about what happened with the others. In addition, they thought it best if they kept a low profile about the part they'd played in it.

"Mrs. Maple wouldn't want to gloat," Madeleine said.

I was wondering how to start when Sandra Elliott made it easy by asking where the mother-daughter pair were. "About that," I said and then launched into the whole story. They were all stunned when they realized someone in their midst had been the killer.

The discussion turned to what would happen to them now. Since I was dealing with a lot of mystery fans, they seemed to know the answer, or at least what they thought the answer was.

Everyone agreed that something would be done to protect Emily and maybe even an identity change. Everyone thought that Jenn Pomelo Van Ness Peltier would be charged with murder. Some of them thought she might claim self-defense and work out a deal if she finally testified in the Ruggio case. But it seemed likely that she'd be spending time in jail in some kind of protective custody.

"Everybody thought it was Brook Tanner," Sandra Elliott said. "She sure seemed guilty with all the mystery connected to her."

"I did a little investigating this morning and I think I figured something out. She was married to an older man who had been married three times. Each time the marriages lasted about seven years and the women were all in their thirties. She's been married to him for eight years," I said. "She has been coming to Vista Del Mar periodically for a couple of years claiming it was a spiritual retreat. Everybody including her husband assumed she was meeting a guy. It was about more than just jealousy for him. They must have a prenup that says she would get nothing in a divorce if she cheated on him."

They were all watching me with rapt attention. "The way she was dressed in the sweats and baseball cap, it almost seemed like she really was on some sort of spiritual retreat. But then I remembered something." I went into my stop at the twenty-four-hour pharmacy to check if they had postcards and the clerk mentioning a prescription Brook hadn't picked up. I let it sit for a minute before I continued. "It wasn't hard to do some checking. This is a small town and all. The clerk gave me the name of the doctor who prescribed the drug, and as soon as I found out what kind of doctor she was, the whole story fell into place." I took another pause and Bruce Elliott started waving his hand in a circle to get me to speed it up.

"You have our attention. Get to the punch line," he said.

"Okay, the doctor is a dermatologist and I think Brook's been coming here for cosmetic treatments hoping to keep the marriage going on longer than the seven years of the others. That would explain why her face was puffy and why she kept herself hidden with the cap and the loose clothes while she healed. I'm guessing that it didn't work and that her husband is ready for wife number four and was hoping to catch her with someone, which is why he hired Gary Moser."

"Wow," Mary Smith said. Then they all gave me a smattering of applause.

"It's fun following the clues, isn't it?" I said. They all nodded in agreement and I felt like the spider inviting the fly into my web. "I was hoping you all would feel that way," I said. "Because the chalk outline and clues are all still there. Everybody is available for you to question. It's not too late."

"She's right," Victor Ackroyd said. "We might as well do the mystery now." The others agreed and were starting to get up when I stopped them.

"But first, this is the last chance you have to get help with the hand warmers," I said, gesturing to Crystal. It was a little anticlimactic, but they all sat down and took out their knitting. For the rest of the time, they all worked diligently with no talking and everyone had at least one hand warmer completed.

As soon as the hour was up, they all took off to look at the clues and start the hunt for the answer. Madeleine and Milton Carruthers stayed behind to talk to me. "After what Milton and I went through with the real mystery, we feel we might have an unfair advantage to solving what happened to the magician. We thought we'd let them have the fun and we'll stay in the background," Madeleine said. Milton nodded in agreement.

"I thought we could go for a walk on the beach to give them all a head start," Milton said. "And to give me a little alone time with Madeleine." He sounded as though he was really fond of her and I wanted to believe he liked her, not who she was and what she had. I almost pulled him aside to ask him, but then I wondered what I would do with the information if it was bad news. Seeing how happy Madeleine was, would I want to be the one to ruin it for her?

After Frank's suggestion that I have them try to solve the mystery again, I had spread the word that the players needed to be available for questioning. They had all jumped back into action. I was sorry that Cloris wasn't there to play her part and had to get Ned to take her place, which put a different spin on the romance thing. As expected, Kevin St. John had balked, though he ended up giving in.

I was glad that my people were finally working on solving the mystery that had taken so much effort to organize. It was set up so they would spend all their time pursuing a red herring and then the last clue would lead them to the magician's killer.

The feeling of having a hangover was largely gone by now and I had a clear head as I thought over things. I hoped that Crystal would be able to talk the Delacorte sisters into overruling Kevin St. John. It was hard to think of Vista Del Mar without her. It was sad to think about Emily and her mother. I understood how Jenn Van Ness might have looked at what she'd done as self-defense, but I had to believe there could have been another way.

With everybody taken care of for the moment, I went home to make a batch of blond brownies for a last afternoon tea we were serving as the wrap-up. The plan was that all the suspects would be there and the group would present their findings on who the murderer was. Sammy had been lying low all weekend, since it felt wrong to him to have the victim hanging around even when they'd lost interest in the staged crime.

I cut through the Lodge and saw that Brook Tanner was in the seating area looking at a magazine. The hat was off, but she was still in sweats. I couldn't help myself. I had to find out if everything I'd figured was right.

The way she was turning the pages on the magazine, she seemed angry. The obvious thing was to ask her if everything was all right. She glared at me and then seemed as if she was glad to have someone to talk to. "All that I went through to please him," she said, shaking her head with regret. "Do you have any idea how unpleasant those acid peels are." It seemed a rhetorical question so I just nodded. "I won't be coming back here anymore. No need to have a room near the driveway so I can slip in and out without the whole world seeing that my face is a mess. No need to hide out for a couple of weeks either." She looked down at some papers sticking out of a manila envelope. "Divorce papers," she said. "I can't compete with the skin of a twenty-five-year-old." The door opened and a man looked in and she waved. It was the man I'd seen sitting across the table from her in the dining hall. They'd seemed like strangers then, but not anymore. Her expression softened and she smiled as he came toward her. "Maybe it'll work out better with someone my own age."

• • •

I had the wheeled bin with me when I returned to Vista Del Mar and brought the tin of blondies to the parlor in the Gulls building. Lucinda was there with Tag. Since the restaurant was closed on Sunday, he was helping her set up. He took the tin of sweets. They'd already set up the three-tiered stands with plates of finger sandwiches.

The Ackroyds, the Elliotts, Rose Wilburn and Mary Smith came in together. They were all smiles as they put their heads together and talked about their solution. Madeleine and Milton Carruthers trailed behind them. Then the suspects came in and took a similar formation to the reception line at the beginning of the retreat.

Kevin St. John had the first position. Ned was in Cloris's spot and looked like he was going to fall asleep. Tag seemed disconcerted when

Lucinda took the next spot. Bob the barista slipped in. Cory was all smiles when he stood next to Jane the housekeeper.

No surprise, Bruce Elliott was the spokesman for the group and he went through all the steps they'd taken to figure out who had taken out the magician. "It always came back to El Bosso, who was a crime lord and who the magician had cheated," he said. He looked at Kevin St. John in an accusing manner. "You were the likely one. You looked the part and we'd heard the name El Bosso tossed around when you were present. But then when we came across the silver button, we realized that El Bosso wasn't who we thought." Bruce turned and pointed an accusing finger. "It's you," he said, looking at Cory.

"You're right," I said, giving them a hand. Cory didn't know quite what to do, so he took a bow. Sammy came in from the side and joined all of them as they took bows. Then my people took bows. Soon everybody was applauding each other.

After that, they descended on the table of goodies. Kevin St. John spent a moment with Madeleine and then left, taking Ned with him, and sent Bob back to the café. Lucinda and Tag joined the rest by getting plates of food. Jane reminded everyone that her real name was Page and thanked me for including her in the charade. Sammy circulated and entertained with some card tricks.

It was the last time for my group to be together and they began recapping the weekend. The rumble dance seemed to have been a highlight. Madeleine thanked them all for being part of her team of detectives. Then Rose Wilburn showed off some pictures she'd taken. They were all arrangements of things rather than regular photographs.

She had a picture from the beach that had a shoe and then footsteps. Another had a formation of some rocks and seaweed that looked like a face. There were plates of food from the teas, and a whimsical one she'd gotten of a woman's hair blowing behind her that mimicked the horizontal foliage of one the cypress trees behind her.

"It's what I do," she said. "I post arrangements of things on social media. Sometimes they're plays on words, or they have a hidden message. I'm known for them." She let out a heavy sigh. "But it's become an obsession. I am addicted to the comments from all my followers. As long as they're positive." Her expression tensed. "I get too upset when anyone says anything negative. That's why I came here. I wanted to see what happened if I was cut off for a few days." She took a breath and smiled. "It was a little rocky at first, but I think I can moderate myself now."

Her mention of pictures made me think of the one I'd found of me with a plastic sword stuck in it. I asked her about it and she put her face in her hands. "So that's what happened to it. It was nothing personal. I just used a random picture of someone. I thought of it as an arrangement of a victim within a victim. I promise I won't post it."

Mary Smith was watching it all and had her computer out and was typing something in. I tried to get behind her to see what it was, but she closed the computer. Then she turned to face me. "Okay, I might as well come clean now. My name is Matilda Sasco and I'm a travel blogger and reviewer for *Time to Travel* magazine. I go incognito when I'm working on a review in the interest of fair reporting." She looked over the group. "I always try to get information for multiple pieces. I was working on a review of this particular mystery weekend and Vista Del Mar in general. I was asking Gary Moser about traveling solo at a place like this when he asked me to bring him into the tea. It was not a date."

I wondered about her wandering around the area behind the registration counter in the Lodge and she said she wanted to see if there really wasn't any WiFi. She'd looked at the clues early because of what she was writing.

I wanted them to have a memento, so I took some group pictures with each of their phones with their hands on top of each other, all wearing one of the hand warmers. And then it was time to go. There were all the final goodbyes and promises to keep in touch. I saw Madeleine standing by as Milton got in his car. Then it was just the two of us watching as the cars went up the driveway and out between the stone pillars back into the real world.

"Well," I said, "was it what you'd hoped for?"

She let out a wistful sigh. "That and more. Though I can't wait to get back into my jeans."

• • •

By Sunday night everything seemed back to normal. I packed up the ingredients for the muffins and headed to downtown Cadbury. Everything but the twenty-four-hour pharmacy was closed and my Mini Cooper was the only car parked on Grand Street.

Because the restaurant was closed on Sunday, there was no chef to trade glances with or having to watch Tag reset the tables. I put on the soft jazz and went into the kitchen and started to pull out the ingredients for a pumpkin spice Bundt cake now that Halloween was coming up. I thought of how much fun it was going to be to have kids in costumes coming to my door.

I recognized Dane's tap at the door and went to let him in. It seemed like a century ago since I'd seen him at the dance, but it was only the night before. He was finally off duty after the extra shift he'd gotten and was back in his jeans and T-shirt.

It was nice having his company and finally to have a peaceful moment, though I already knew it wasn't going to last.

"Anything new?" he said as a joke.

"So much to tell," I said, glad I had someone to share it with. "Tag is in a tizzy because he found the missing cup wasn't broken. Kevin St. John is upset because Crystal has already gotten Madeleine and Cora sympathetic to Cloris, and he's blaming it all on me. I found out the origin of the picture of me with a pierced heart and it was nothing. But I also found out one of the retreaters was writing a review of the weekend. She wouldn't give me a hint if it is good or bad. I have to wait to see it in print. Whatever was going on between Madeleine and Milton Carruthers isn't over and I'm still not sure of his intentions.

She told me he's coming back for a writers' retreat at Vista Del Mar next month. I promised Crystal to plan a girls' night with her, Cloris and Lucinda. Now I realize I have to include Madeleine. The final bit of news . . ." I shook my head with dismay. "I hope you're ready for a bumpy ride ahead." I paused from measuring the flour. "My parents announced they're coming for a visit."

He rolled his eyes as he went to open the cans of pumpkin. "Wow, that is a lot. I guess that means living together is off the table for now," he said with a grin to let me know he was teasing. "But you know me. I'll be here for whatever."

It was nice to know that he wasn't teasing about that.

Crystal's Hand Warmers

This is an easy knit pattern that is one size fits most.

Materials:

5.00/size 8 needles
1 skein Lion Brand Ferris Wheel Yarn, 3oz/85g, 270 yd/247m, 100% acrylic, 4 weight—for the blended but not matched pair. It's enough yarn to make a pair with yarn left over.
1 skein Lion Brand Heartland Yarn, 5oz/142 grams, 251 yd/230m, 4 weight—for the solid color matched pair. It's enough to make a pair with yarn left over.
Tapestry needle

Instructions:

Cast on 32 stitches
Row 1: Knit across.
Row 2: knit across
Row 3: knit2 purl2 across row
Repeat Row 3 until the piece is 6 inches in length.

Cast off leaving a long tail.

Starting with the cast-off row as the top, use the tapestry needle and the long tail to sew together the sides for one inch. Leave an opening of 1½ inch for thumb hole and sew the rest together. Fasten off and weave in the loose strands

Make 2

Casey's Favorite Banana Nut Muffins

Line muffin tin with paper baking cups. Preheat oven to 350F.

Ingredients:

⅓ cup olive oil
1 cup sugar
2 large eggs, beaten
¼ cup milk
1 teaspoon vanilla
3 medium bananas, very ripe, mashed
2 cups all-purpose flour
1 teaspoon baking soda
¼ teaspoon salt
½ cup chopped nuts

In a large bowl, whisk together olive oil and sugar. Add eggs and whisk until completely combined. Add milk and vanilla, whisk. Add flour, baking soda and salt and, using a spoon or spatula, stir just until no more dry flour is visible. Fold in nuts. Fill paper baking cups ¾ full. Bake 20–25 min or until a tooth pick comes out clean.

Makes 12

Afternoon Tea Sour Cream Biscuits

Line a baking sheet with parchment paper. Preheat oven 425F.

Ingredients:

2 cups all-purpose flour
1 tablespoon baking powder
1 teaspoon salt
16-ounce container of sour cream
7 tablespoons butter, melted and cooled

Combine flour, baking powder and salt in a bowl. Stir in sour cream and 5 tablespoons of butter until combined. Two soup spoons work well to combine the sour cream and butter with the dry ingredients.

Drop scoops (soup spoons are good for this too) of the dough on the paper-lined baking sheet about 2 inches apart.

Drizzle the other two tablespoons of butter over the biscuits before placing in the oven.

Bake 20–25 minutes, until golden brown. Halfway through, turn the pan around.

Cool on a rack.

Delicious on their own or could be served with honey, jam with or without clotted cream.

Makes 12

About the Author

Betty Hechtman is the national bestselling author of the Crochet Mysteries and the Yarn Retreat Mysteries. Handicrafts and writing are her passions and she is thrilled to be able to combine them in both of her series. She also writes the Writer for Hire Mysteries, which are set in her Chicago neighborhood of Hyde Park and have a touch of crochet.

Betty grew up on the South Side of Chicago and has a degree in Fine Art. Since College, she has studied everything from improv comedy to magic. She has had an assortment of professions, including volunteer farm worker picking fruit on a kibbutz tucked between Lebanon and Syria, nanny at a summer resort, waitress at a coffee house, telephone operator, office worker at the Writer's Guild, public relations assistant at a firm with celebrity clients, and newsletter editor at a Waldorf school. She has written newspaper and magazine pieces, short stories, screenplays, and a middle-grade mystery, *Stolen Treasure*. She lives with her family and stash of yarn in Southern California.

See BettyHechtman.com for more information, excerpts from all her books, and photos of all the projects of the patterns included in her books. She blogs on Fridays at Killerhobbies.blogspot.com, and you can join her on Facebook at BettyHechtmanAuthor.

Made in the USA
Coppell, TX
04 March 2023

13783497R00135